Issues for Today

An Intermediate Reading Skills Text

Second Edition

Issues for Today

An Intermediate Reading Skills Text

Second Edition

Lorraine C. Smith
Nancy Nici Mare

English Language Institute
Queens College
The City University of New York

Illustrations by
Joseph Tenga

Heinle & Heinle Publishers
I(T)P A Division of International Thomson Publishing, Inc.
Boston, Massachusetts 02116 U.S.A.

The ITP logo is a trademark under license.

Pacific Grove • Albany • Bonn • Boston • Cincinnati • Detroit • London • Madrid • Melbourne
Mexico City • New York • Paris • San Francisco • Tokyo • Toronto • Washington

The publication of *Issues for Today, Second Edition* was directed by members of the Newbury House Publishing Team at Heinle & Heinle:

Erik Gundersen, **Editorial Director**
John F. McHugh, **Market Development Director**
Kristin Thalheimer, **Production Services Coordinator**
Elizabeth Holthaus, **Director of Production and Team Leader**

Also participating in the publication of this program were:
Publisher: Stanley J. Galek
Project Manager: LeGwin Associates
Assistant Editor: Karen P. Hazar
Associate Production Editor: Maryellen Eschmann
Manufacturing Coordinator: Mary Beth Hennebury
Cover Designer: Kim Wedlake

Heinle & Heinle Publishers
20 Park Plaza
Boston, MA 02116 USA

International Thomson Publishing
Berkshire House 168-173
High Holborn
London WC1V 7AA
England

Thomas Nelson Australia
102 Dodds Street
South Melbourne, 3205
Victoria, Australia

Nelson Canada
1120 Birchmount Road
Scarborough, Ontario
Canada M1K 5G1

International Thomson Publishing Gmbh
Konigwinterer Strasse 418
53227 Bonn
Germany

International Thomson Publishing Asia
Block 311 Henderson Road #08-03
Henderson Industrial Park
Singapore 0315

International Thomson Publishing-Japan
Hirakawacho-cho Kyowa Building, 3F
2-2-1 Hirakawacho-cho
Chiyoda-ku, 102 Tokyo
Japan

All art and illustration by Joseph Tenga except as noted below:
Photos on pps. 45, 100 and 113: Jonathan Stark/Heinle & Heinle Publishers.
Photo on p. 26: © Tom McCarthy/PhotoEdit.
Photo on p. 128: UPI/Bettmann.
Photo on p. 167: The Granger Collection.
Photo on p. 183 courtesy of Jet Propulsion Laboratory.

Library of Congress Cataloging-in-Publication Data
Smith, Lorraine C.
Issues for today: an intermediate reading skills text/Lorraine C. Smith, Nancy Nici Mare; illustrations by Joseph Tenga.—2nd. ed.
p. cm.
"English Language Institute, Queens College, The City University of New York."
ISBN 0-8384-5025-3
1. English language—Textbooks for foreign speakers 2. Reading (Adult education) I. Mare, Nancy Nici. 1957. II. Queens College (New York, N.Y.). English Language Institute. III. Title.
PE1128.S5844 1994
428.6'4–dc20 94–41255
CIP

5 6 7 8 9 10 XXX 01 00 99 98

Contents

Preface

Issues for Today, Second Edition is a reading skills textbook intended for intermediate, academically-oriented students of English as a second or foreign language. The passages in this thematically-organized book introduce students to topics of universal interest. As students work with the materials in each chapter, they develop the kinds of extensive and intensive reading skills they will need to achieve academic success in English.

Issues for Today is one in a series of reading skills texts. The complete series has been designed to meet the needs of students from the beginning to the advanced levels and includes the following:

- *Themes for Today* .... beginning
- *Insights for Today* .... high beginning
- *Issues for Today* .... intermediate
- *Concepts for Today* .... high intermediate
- *Topics for Today* .... advanced

Issues for Today consists of four sections. Each section contains three chapters that deal with related subjects. At the same time, each chapter is an independent unit, entirely separate in content from the other two chapters contained in that section. This gives the instructor the option of either completing entire sections or choosing individual chapters as a focus in class.

All of the chapters provide the students with interesting and stimulating topics to read, think about, and discuss. The initial exercises are an introduction to each reading passage and encourage the students to think about the ideas, facts, and vocabulary that will be presented. The exercises which follow the reading passage are intended to improve reading comprehension skills as well as comprehension of English sentence structure. The activities will help them see relationships between parts of a sentence, between sentences, and between and within paragraphs. The articles contain useful vocabulary which the students can use in the real world and the exercises are designed to sharpen their ability to learn vocabulary from context. Students should learn not to rely on a bilingual dictionary. A word form exercise is included in each chapter to help students develop a "feel" for the patterns of word forms in English and an awareness of morphemes, for example, the suffix -tion always indicates a noun. Many vocabulary and word form selections are repeated in subsequent chapters to provide reinforcement.

The progression of exercises and activities in each chapter leads the students through general comprehension of main ideas, specific information, understanding structural details, and specific vocabulary. Since reading college material also involves note-taking skills, students are trained to outline the article via diagrams, charts and outlines, and to briefly summarize the passage. Finally, the students practice manipulating new vocabulary by working with their different parts of speech, and varying the tense in both affirmative and negative forms, and singular and plural forms.

New to the Second Edition

While *Issues for Today, Second Edition* retains the overall format of the first edition, the authors have made several significant changes to the original book. The second edition contains four new chapters: "Dreams: Making Them Work for Us," "Language: Is It Always Spoken?" "Innocent Until Proven Guilty: The Criminal Court System," and "How Lunar Eclipses Have Changed History." In addition, several of the original readings have been updated to reflect new information.

Issues for Today, Second Edition contains an enhanced Prereading Preparation section, which contains more thoughtful, motivating questions and activities. The second edition includes improved graphics, which are accompanied by questions designed to enhance students' comprehension of information presented in graphs. The Notetaking Outline exercise has been redesigned. The new Information Organization exercise includes outlines, charts and flowcharts, depending on each reading and the type of information it contains. This tailoring of the organization of information will make the Reading Recall, formerly called Comprehension Questions, a more purposeful activity. Furthermore, the Information Organization design takes into account students' different learning and organizational styles. The new Follow-Up Activities section contains a variety of activities, and provides more opportunities for discussion and interaction. Moreover, *Issues for Today, Second Edition* contains surveys, which provide students with the means and the opportunity to go out into the "real world" and interact with native English speakers in meaningful ways, and affords them the opportunity to collect data that they can bring back to class and combine, generating graphs of their own for interpretation and discussion. *Issues for Today, Second Edition* includes end-of-unit crossword puzzles, which provide a review of the vocabulary encountered in all three chapters of each unit, and Unit Discussion questions, which help students think about, discuss, and make connections among the topics in the chapters of each unit.

All of these revisions and enhancements to *Issues for Today, Second Edition* have been designed to help students improve their reading skills and develop confidence as they work through the text. At the same time, the second edition is structured so that the students will steadily progress towards skillful, independent reading.

Acknowledgments

The authors gratefully acknowledge all our friends and colleagues at the ELI at Queens College for their ongoing help, ideas, and suggestions for the revision of this manuscript. We are also very grateful to the teachers and students everywhere who, because of their tremendous support of the first edition of this book, made this second edition a reality. We wish to thank Kristin Thalheimer, our Production Editor, for her help and hard work. Once again, we want to express our appreciation to our very patient editor, Erik Gundersen, for his continued faith in our work.

L.C.S. and N.N.M.

Introduction

How to Use This Book

Each chapter in this book consists of the following:

Prereading Preparation
Reading Passage
Fact-Finding Exercise
Reading Analysis
Information Organization
Information Recall and Summary
Word Forms
Vocabulary in Context
Topics for Discussion and Writing
Follow-up Activities

Chapters 7–12 also include a Dictionary Skills exercise. Each unit contains a crossword puzzle, which incorporates vocabulary from all three chapters in the unit. The discussion section at the end of each unit ties in the related topics of the three chapters. There is a CLOZE quiz for each chapter located in the Pullout Section at the end of the book. This gives the teacher the option of removing the entire test section from all the students' books at the beginning of the term and giving out each test as the class finishes each chapter. The Answer Key is at the end of the Pullout Section and may also be removed by the teacher at the beginning of the term, along with the CLOZE tests.

Prereading Preparation

This prereading activity is designed to stimulate student interest and provide preliminary vocabulary for the passage itself. The importance of prereading preparation should not be underestimated. Studies have shown the positive effect of prereading preparation in motivating student interest, activating background knowledge, and enhancing reading comprehension. Time should be spent describing and discussing the illustrations as well as discussing the chapter title and the prereading questions. Furthermore, students should try to relate the topic to their own experience and try to predict what they are going to read about.

Reading Passage

The students will read the passage for the first time. They should be instructed to time themselves and to try to aim for a higher reading speed the second time they read the passage. They should also be encouraged to read *ideas*, not just words.

Fact-Finding Exercise

After reading the passage again, the students will read the True/False statements and check whether they are true or false. If the statement is false, the students will rewrite the statement so that it is true. They will then go back to the passage and find the line(s) that contain the correct answer. This activity can be done individually or in groups.

Reading Analysis

The students will read each question and answer it. The first question in this section always refers to the main idea. There are three possible answers. Two answers are incorrect because they are too general or too narrow, they are not mentioned in the passage, or they are false. When going over the exercise, the teacher should discuss with the students why the other two answers are incorrect. The rest of this exercise requires the students to think about the structure of the sentences and paragraphs, and the relationships of ideas to each other. This exercise is very effective when done in groups. It may also be done individually, but if done in groups it gives the students an excellent opportunity to discuss possible answers.

Information Organization

In this exercise, the students are asked to read the passage again, take notes, and organize the information they have just read. They may be asked to complete an outline, a table, or a flowchart. The teacher may want to review the concept of notetaking before beginning the exercise. The outline, table, or flowchart can be sketched on the blackboard by the teacher or a student and completed by individual students in front of the class. Variations can be discussed by the class as a group. It should be pointed out to students that in American colleges, teachers often base their exams on the notes that the students are expected to take during class lectures, and that they, too, will be tested on their notes.

Information Recall and Summary

The questions in this exercise are based on the notes the students took in the Information Organization exercise. Students should be instructed to read the questions and then to refer to their notes to answer them. They are also asked to write a summary of the article. The teacher may want to review how to summarize at the beginning of the class. This section can be prepared in class and discussed. Alternately, it can be assigned for homework.

Word Forms

As an introduction to the word form exercises in this book, it is recommended that the teacher first review parts of speech, especially verbs, nouns, adjectives, and adverbs. Teachers should point out each word form's position in a sentence. Students will develop a sense for which part of speech is missing in a given sentence. Teachers should also point out clues to tense and number, and whether an idea is affirmative or negative. Each section has its own instructions, depending on the particular pattern that is being introduced. For example, in the section containing words that take *-tion* in the noun form, the teacher can explain that in this exercise the students will look at the verb and noun forms of two types of words that use the suffix *-tion* in their noun form. (1) Some words simply add *-tion* to the verb: *convict\conviction*; if the word ends in *e*, the *e* is dropped first: *execute/execution*; (2) other words drop the final *e* and add *-ation*: *combine\combination*. This exercise is very effective when done in pairs. After students have a working knowledge of this type of exercise, it can be assigned for homework.

Dictionary Skills

This exercise, in Chapters 7–12, provides students with much-needed practice in selecting the appropriate dictionary entry for an unknown word, depending on the context. Students are given entries from the *Oxford ESL Dictionary*. The sentence containing the dictionary word is provided above the entry. After selecting the appropriate entry, the student rewrites the sentence using the chosen definition. The students should write the answer in a grammatically correct form, as they may not always copy verbatim from the dictionary. The students can work in pairs on this exercise and report back to the class. They should be prepared to justify their choices.

Vocabulary in Context

This is a fill-in exercise designed as a review of the items in the previous exercises. The vocabulary has been covered either in the questions or the Reading Analysis section. It can be done for homework as a review or in class as group work.

Topics for Discussion and Writing

In this section, students are encouraged to use the information and vocabulary from the passage both orally and in writing. The writing assignment may be done in class or at home.

Follow-Up Activities

This section contains various activities appropriate to the information in the passages. Some activities are designed for pair and small-group work. Students are encouraged to use the information and vocabulary from the passages both orally and in writing. The teacher may also use these questions and activities as home or in-class assignments.

Index of Key Words and Phrases

This section contains words and phrases from all the chapters, for easy reference. It is located after the last chapter, before the pullout section.

Pullout Section

CLOZE

The CLOZE quiz not only tests vocabulary, but also sentence structure and comprehension in general. The quiz is a modified version of the reading passage itself, with 20 items to be completed. At the top of the answer page, students are given the 20 words to be filled in the blank spaces. The quiz for each chapter is placed at the end of the book in the Pullout Section. The teacher has the option of collecting the entire Pullout Section of quizzes, including the Answer Key, from students at the beginning of the semester. In this way, the teacher will have a copy of all the quizzes for each student in the class and can administer the quizzes after each unit is covered. The quizzes can be done either as a test or as a group assignment.

Answer Key

The Answer Key can be found in a separate edition of *Issues for Today, Second Edition* (ISBN: 0-8384-5025-3).

Unit I

Trends in Living

C · H · A · P · T · E · R 1

A Cultural Difference: Being on Time

• Prereading Preparation

1. What does **on time** mean?

2. Is it always important to be on time? Look at the table below. How important is it to be on time for each appointment? Put a check mark in the box to show your answer. Discuss your answers with the class.

How Important Is It . . .?

Type of Appointment	Scheduled Time	Very Important	Slightly Important	Not Important
dentist	9 A.M.			
university class	11 A.M.			
lunch with a friend at school	12 P.M.			
dinner with your spouse	7 P.M.			
a friend's party	9 P.M.			
job interview in a bank	2 P.M.			

3. Are you usually on time, or are you usually late? Why?

4. Read the title of the article. What do you think this article is about?

1 In the United States, it is important to be on time, or
2 punctual, for an appointment, a class, a meeting, etc.
3 However, this may not be true in all countries. An
4 American professor discovered this difference while
5 teaching a class in a Brazilian university. The two-hour
6 class was scheduled to begin at 10 A.M. and end at 12 P.M.
7 On the first day, when the professor arrived on time, no

one was in the classroom. Many students came after 10 A.M. Several arrived after 10:30 A.M. Two students came after 11 A.M. Although all the students greeted the professor as they arrived, few apologized for their lateness. Were these students being rude? He decided to study the students' behavior.

The professor talked to American and Brazilian students about lateness in both an informal and a formal situation: lunch with a friend and in a university class, respectively. He gave them an example and asked them how they would react. If they had a lunch appointment with a friend, the average American student defined lateness as 19 minutes after the agreed time. On the other hand, the average Brazilian student felt the friend was late after 33 minutes.

In an American university, students are expected to arrive at the appointed hour. In contrast, in Brazil, neither the teacher nor the students always arrive at the appointed hour. Classes not only begin at the scheduled time in the United States, but they also end at the scheduled time. In the Brazilian class, only a few students left the class at noon; many remained past 12:30 to discuss the class and ask more questions. While arriving late may not be very important in Brazil, neither is staying late.

The explanation for these differences is complicated. People from Brazilian and North American cultures have different feelings about lateness. In Brazil, the students believe that a person who usually arrives late is probably more successful than a person who is always on time. In fact, Brazilians expect a person with status or prestige to arrive late, while in the United States lateness is usually considered to be disrespectful and unacceptable. Consequently, if a Brazilian is late for an appointment with a North American, the American may misinterpret the reason for the lateness and become angry.

As a result of his study, the professor learned that the Brazilian students were not being disrespectful to him. Instead, they were simply behaving in the appropriate way for a Brazilian student in Brazil. Eventually, the professor was able to adapt his own behavior so that he could feel comfortable in the new culture.

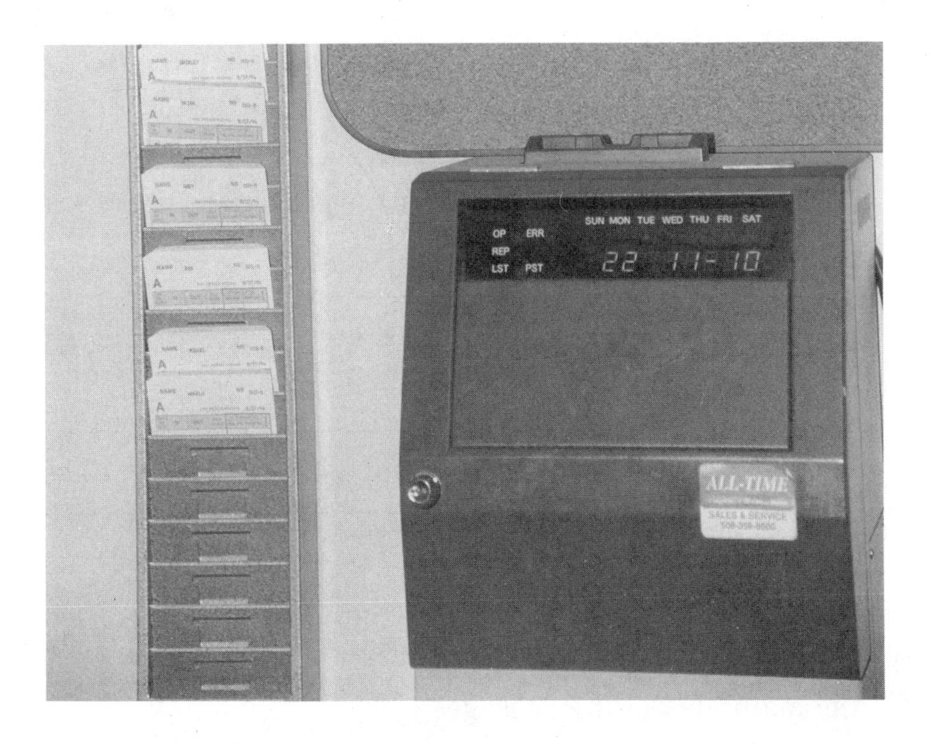

• A. Fact-Finding Exercise

Read the passage again. Read the following statements. Check whether they are True (T) or False (F). If a statement is false, rewrite the statement so that it is true. Then go back to the passage and find the line that supports your answer.

______ T ______ F 1. On the first day of class, the professor arrived late, but the students were on time.

____

______ T ______ F 2. The professor decided to study the behavior of Brazilian and American students.

____

______ T ______ F 3. In an American university, it is important to be on time.

____

______ T ______ F 4. In a Brazilian class, the students leave immediately after the class is finished.

____

______ T ______ F 5. In an American university, many students probably leave immediately after the class is finished.

____

_____ T _____ F 6. Most North Americans think a person who is late is disrespectful.

____

_____ T _____ F 7. In Brazil, most successful people are expected to be on time.

____

_____ T _____ F 8. As a result of the study, the professor changed the Brazilian students' behavior.

____

• B. Reading Analysis

Read each question carefully. Either circle the letter of the correct answer, or write your answer in the space provided.

1. What is the main idea of the passage?

   a. It is important to be on time for class in the United States.
   b. People learn the importance of time when they are children.
   c. The importance of being on time differs among cultures.

2. Why did the professor study the Brazilian students' behavior?

   a. The students seemed very rude to him.
   b. He wanted to understand why the students came late.
   c. He wanted to make the students come to class on time.

3. a. Read lines 1 and 2. What does **punctual** mean?

   ____

   b. How do you know?

   ____

4. In line 11, what does **few** refer to?

   a. the professor
   b. the students
   c. greetings

5. Read lines 10–13. What is **rude** behavior?

   a. impolite behavior
   b. noisy behavior
   c. studious behavior

6. a. Read lines 14–17. Which is an example of an informal situation?

   ____

   b. Which is an example of a formal situation?

   ____

   c. How do you know?

   ____

   d. What does this word mean?

      1. the same as
      2. in the same order
      3. opposite

7. In lines 20 and 21, how does **on the other hand** connect the American idea of lateness with the Brazilian idea of lateness?

   a. It shows a similarity.
   b. It gives more information.
   c. It shows a contrast.

8. Read lines 24–26: "neither the teacher nor the students always arrive at the appointed hour." Who arrives at the appointed hour?

   a. no one
   b. the students only
   c. the teacher and the students

9. Read lines 26–28: "Classes not only begin at the scheduled time in the United States, but they also end at the scheduled time." What does **not only . . . but . . . also** mean?

   a. and
   b. but
   c. so

10. In line 38, what does **in fact** indicate?

    a. a contrast between two ideas
    b. something that is true
    c. emphasis of the previous idea

11. Read lines 45–48. What does **instead** show?

    a. a similarity
    b. a substitution
    c. an opposite

• C. Information Organization

Read the passage again. Underline what you think are the main ideas. Then scan the reading and complete the following flowchart, using the sentences that you have underlined to help you. You will use this flowchart later to answer questions about the reading.

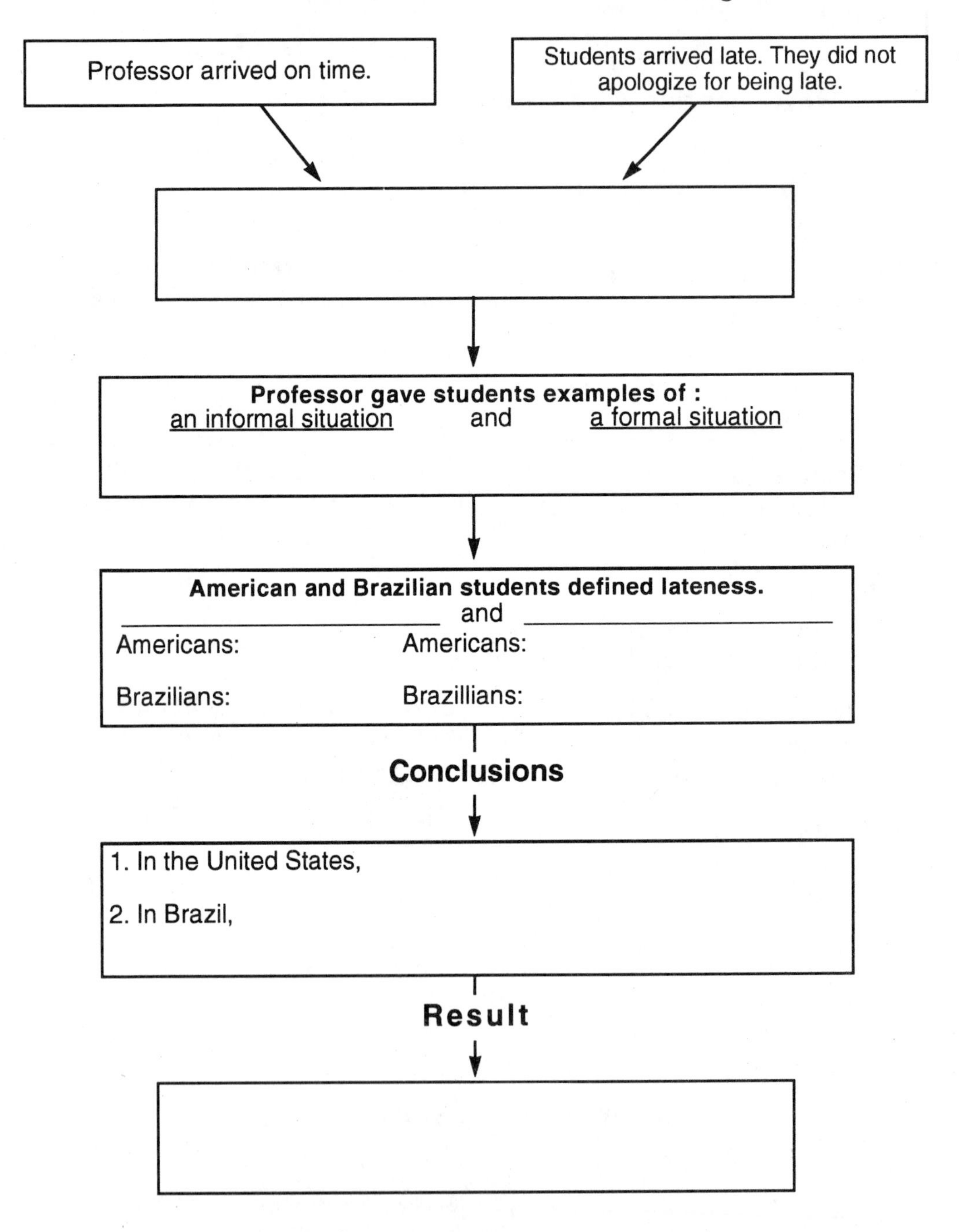

• D. Information Recall and Summary

Read each question carefully. Use your flowchart to answer the questions. Do not refer back to the passage. When you are finished, write a brief summary of the reading.

1. What did the professor decide to study?

   ____

2. Describe the professor's experiment.

   ____

   ____

3. Did American students and Brazilian students have the same ideas about lateness in class? Do classes always begin and end at the appointed hour in both cultures?

   ____

   ____

4. What were the American students' and the Brazilian students' ideas about being late for a lunch appointment?

   ____

   ____

5. In general, what did the Brazilian students think about people who are late?

   ____

6. In general, what did the American students think about people who are late?

   ____

7. What was the result of the professor's study?

   ____

Summary

Work in pairs or alone. Write a brief summary of the reading, and put it on the blackboard. Compare your summary with your classmates'. Which one best describes the main idea of the reading?

____

____

____

____

• E. Word Forms

Part 1

In English, verbs change to nouns in several ways. Some verbs become nouns by adding the suffix *-ing*—for example, *feel* (v.) becomes *feeling* (n.).

Complete each sentence with the correct form of the words on the left. **Use the correct tense of the verb in either the affirmative or the negative form. Use the singular or plural form of the noun.**

spell (v.) spelling (n.)	1. a. Allen ________________ several words incorrectly on his composition yesterday. b. He has to check the ________________ of a difficult word before he uses it.
understand (v.) understanding (n.)	2. a. Andrew ________________ anything in his first math class yesterday. b. However, his ________________ will improve during the semester.
end (v.) ending (n.)	3. a. Please don't tell me the ________________ of this mystery story. b. I want to guess how the story ____________ by myself.
greet (v.) greeting (n.)	4. a. "Hi," "Hello," and "How are you" are common ________________ in the United States. b. Most people ________________ each other with a smile.
meet (v.) meeting (n.)	5. a. Our department has ten monthly ________________ every year. b. We ________________ during May or December.

Part 2

In English, verbs change to nouns in several ways. Some verbs become nouns by adding the suffix *-ation*—for example—*combine* (v.), becomes *combination* (n.).

Complete each sentence with the correct form of the words on the left. **Use the correct tense of the verb in either the affirmative or the negative form. Use the singular or plural form of the noun**.

adapt (v.) adaptation (n.)	1. a. Next year a big film company __________ a story from a book to make a movie. b. The __________ of a book to a movie takes a lot of work and time.
interpret (v.) interpretation (n.)	2. a. Chris is studying at the university for a degree in __________. b. When he graduates, he __________ for an embassy.
expect (v.) expectation (n.)	3. a. Some people have high __________ when they visit another country. b. They want to enjoy themselves. They __________ to have a bad time.
observe (v.) observation (n.)	4. a. Suzie is in the park now. She __________ the behavior of pigeons. b. She records all her __________ in a special notebook.
explain (v.) explanation (n.)	5. a. We needed an __________ of the difference between adjectives and adverbs. b. The teacher __________ the difference to us, and we understood.

• F. Vocabulary in Context

adapt (v.)
apologized (v.)
appropriate (adj.)
behavior (n.)
greets (v.)
in fact
prestige (n.)
punctual (adj.)
rude (adj.)
unacceptable (adj.)

Read the following sentences. Complete each blank space with the correct word or phrase from the list above. Use each word or phrase only once.

1. A suit and tie are ______________ clothes for a business meeting.
2. Wearing shorts in a church is ______________.
3. In most countries, doctors have considerable ______________. People respect them highly.
4. Greg always ______________ people by smiling and saying hello.
5. It was very ______________ of Martin to ask Mrs. Barnes her age.
6. Being ______________ for a job interview is important in order to make a good impression.
7. When you walk into a dark room from the bright sunlight, your eyes need a few moments to ______________ to the change in light.
8. It is very cold in Antarctica. ______________, it is the coldest place on Earth.
9. Martha dropped chocolate ice cream on my white rug. She ______________, but I told her not to worry about it, and we cleaned it up.
10. I don't understand Mark's ______________. He gets angry for no reason and refuses to talk to anyone.

• G. Topics for Discussion and Writing

1. Describe how people in your culture feel about someone who is late. For example, do you think that person is inconsiderate and irresponsible, or do you think that person is prestigious and successful? Please explain your answer, and also give some examples.

2. How do you think the professor adapted his behavior in Brazil after his study? Why do you think he changed his behavior? Why didn't he try to change the Brazilian students' behavior?

3. In this story, the American professor changed his behavior to adapt to the customs of Brazil. Do you think it is important to adapt your behavior to a new culture? In what ways would you be willing to make changes? Please explain.

• H. Follow-Up Activity

There are many differences in customs among cultures. In the table below, list some cultural differences between this country and your country, or between your country and another country you have visited. Compare your list with your classmates' lists.

Cultural Difference	________ (Your Country)	________ (Other Country)
1. clothes: school work		
2.		
3.		
4.		
5.		

C·H·A·P·T·E·R 2

Changing Lifestyles and New Eating Habits

• Prereading Preparation

1. What are **lifestyles?** Give examples of two very different lifestyles. Describe how they are different.
2. Think about your life today. Is your life different today than it was three or four years ago? Write about some differences in your life now. List them in the chart below, and tell a classmate about them.

My Life Today	My Life 3 or 4 Years Ago

3. How do you think American lifestyles are changing? Read the title of this article. What do you think this article is about? What examples do you think the author will give?

1 Americans today have different eating habits than
2 they had in the past. There is a wide selection of food
3 available. They have a broader knowledge of nutrition,
4 so they buy more fresh fruit and vegetables than ever
5 before. At the same time, Americans purchase increas-
6 ing quantities of sweets, snacks and sodas.
7 Statistics show that the way people live determines
8 the way they eat. American lifestyles have changed.
9 They now include growing numbers of people who live
10 alone, single parents and children, and double-income
11 families. These changing lifestyles are responsible for
12 the increasing number of people who must rush meals
13 or sometimes skip them altogether. Many Americans
14 have less time than ever before to spend preparing
15 food. Partly as a consequence of this limited time, 60%
16 of all American homes now have microwave ovens.

17 Moreover, Americans eat out nearly four times a week
18 on the average.
19 It is easy to study the amounts and kinds of food
20 that people consume. The United States Department of
21 Agriculture (USDA) and the food industry—growers, pro-
22 cessors, marketers, and restaurateurs—compile sales
23 statistics and keep accurate records. This information
24 not only tells us what people are eating, but also tells us
25 about the changes in attitudes and tastes. Red meat,
26 which used to be the most popular choice for dinner, is
27 no longer an American favorite. Instead, chicken, turkey
28 and fish have become more popular. Sales of these
29 foods have greatly increased in recent years. This is
30 probably a result of the awareness of the dangers of eat-
31 ing food that contains high levels of cholesterol, or ani-
32 mal fat. Doctors believe that cholesterol is a threat to
33 human health.
34 According to a recent survey, Americans also change
35 their eating patterns to meet the needs of different situ-
36 ations. They have certain ideas about which foods will
37 increase their athletic ability, help them lose weight,
38 make them alert for business meetings, or put them in
39 the mood for romance. For example, Americans choose
40 pasta, fruit, and vegetables, which supply them with
41 carbohydrates, to give them strength for physical activ-
42 ity, such as sports. Adults choose foods rich in fiber,
43 such as bread and cereal, for breakfast, and salads for
44 lunch to prepare them for business appointments. For
45 romantic dinners, however, Americans choose shrimp
46 and lobster. While many of these ideas are based on nu-
47 tritional facts, some are not.
48 Americans' awareness of nutrition, along with their
49 changing tastes and needs, leads them to consume a
50 wide variety of foods—foods for health, for fun, and
51 simply for good taste.

• A. Fact-Finding Exercise

Read the passage again. Read the following statements. Check whether they are True (T) or False (F). If a statement is false, rewrite the statement so that it is true. Then go back to the passage and find the line that supports your answer.

_____ T _____ F 1. Americans eat the same way they did in the past.

____

_____ T _____ F 2. Americans do not eat many sweets anymore.

____

_____ T _____ F 3. Most Americans do not have a lot of time to prepare food.

____

_____ T _____ F 4. Red meat is the most popular American choice for dinner.

____

_____ T _____ F 5. Americans eat out about four times a week.

____

_____ T _____ F 6. The USDA keeps information about the food Americans buy.

____

_____ T _____ F 7. It is healthy to eat food with high cholesterol levels.

____

_____ T _____ F 8. Americans choose foods rich in fiber for romantic dinners.

____

• B. Reading Analysis

Read each question carefully. Either circle the letter of the correct answer, or write your answer in the space provided.

1. What is the main idea of the passage?

   a. American eating habits have changed because of changing lifestyles.
   b. Americans have a greater awareness of nutrition than they did years ago.
   c. Americans have less time than ever before to prepare meals.

2. In line 5–6, what are **quantities**?

   a. kinds
   b. amounts
   c. types

3. Read lines 8–11.

   a. What are **lifestyles**?

      1. the way people live
      2. the way people eat
      3. the way people dress

   b. What is a **double-income family**?

      1. a family that makes twice as much money as another family
      2. a family in which one adult has two jobs
      3. a family in which two adults work full-time

4. Read lines 17–18. What does **on the average** mean?

   a. exactly
   b. approximately
   c. sometimes

5. In lines 20–23, what are examples of jobs in the food industry?

   ____

6. Read lines 25–28. What is **red meat**?

   a. chicken
   b. fish
   c. beef

7. a. In line 31–32, what is **cholesterol**?

   ____

   b. How do you know?

   ____

8. In line 45, what does **however** indicate?

   a. an explanation
   b. a similarity
   c. a contrast

9. Read lines 46–47.

   a. What does **while** mean?
      1. during
      2. although
      3. also

   b. What does **some** refer to?

      1. ideas
      2. facts
      3. Americans

10. In line 48, what does **along with** mean?

    a. except for
    b. together with
    c. instead of

• C. Information Organization

Read the passage again. Underline what you think are the main ideas. Then scan the reading and complete the following flowchart, using the sentences that you have underlined to help you. You will use this flowchart later to answer questions about the reading.

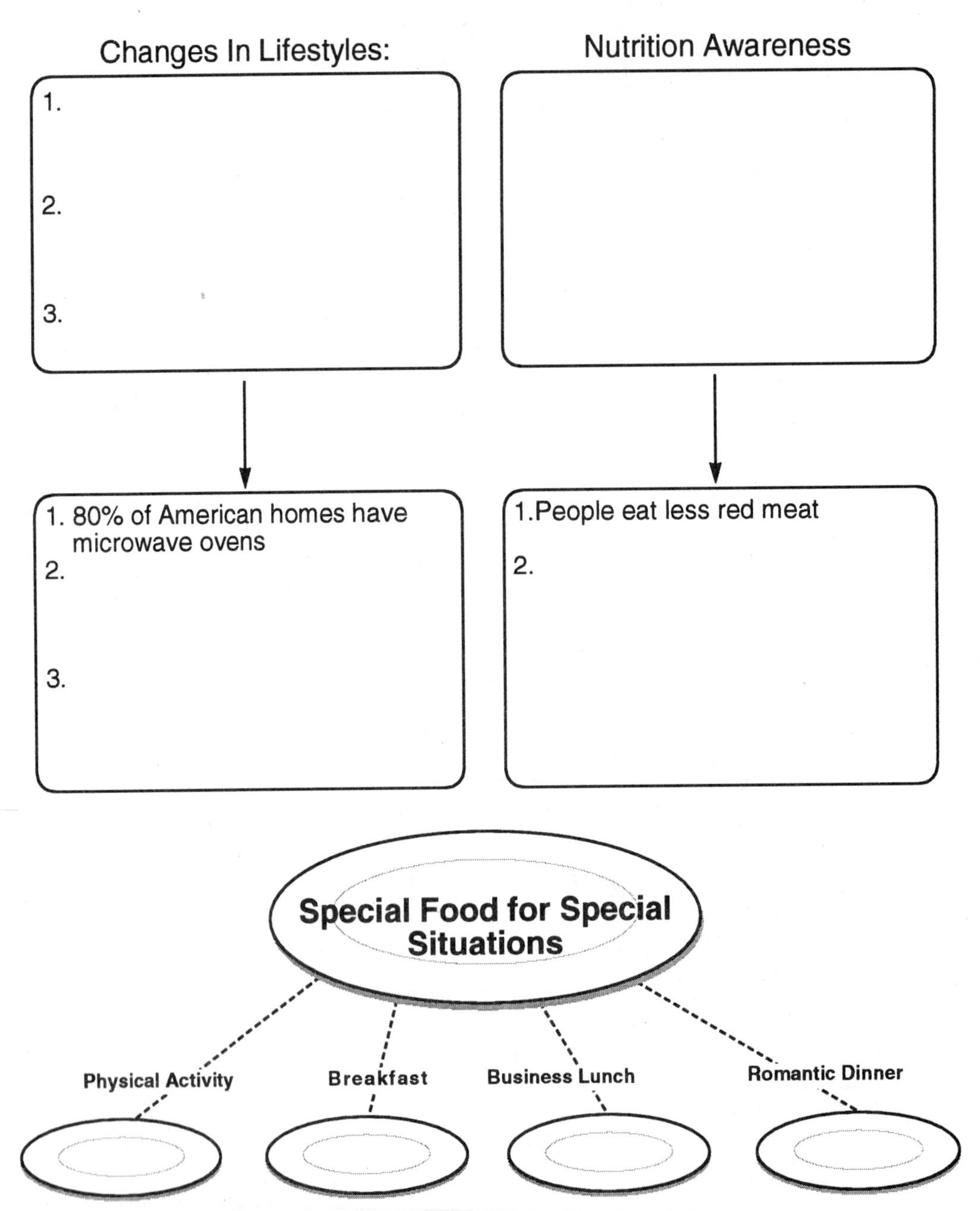

• D. Information Recall and Summary

Read each question carefully. Use your flowchart to answer the questions. Do not refer back to the passage. When you are finished, write a brief summary of the reading.

1. Why do Americans have different eating habits today?

   ____

   ____

2. a. How have American lifestyles changed? Give examples.

   ____

   ____

   b. How do these changing lifestyles affect the way they eat?

   ____

   ____

3. What have Americans learned about cholesterol in food?

   ____

4. How has the awareness of the danger of cholesterol changed what people eat?

   ____

   ____

5. How do people change their eating patterns according to different situations? Give examples.

   ____

   ____

Summary

Work in pairs or alone. Write a brief summary of the reading, and put it on the blackboard. Compare your summary with your classmates'. Which one best describes the main idea of the reading?

____

____

____

____

____

• E. Word Forms

Part 1

In English, verbs change to nouns in several ways. Some verbs become nouns that represent people by adding the suffix *-er,*—for example, *teach* (v.) becomes *teacher* (n.).

Complete each sentence with the correct form of the words on the left. **Use the correct tense of the verb in either the affirmative or the negative form. Use the singular or plural form of the noun.**

grow (v.)
grower (n.)

1. a. Thomas __________ flowers in his garden. He only plants vegetables.
   b. He is an expert, so other __________ in his neighborhood often ask him for advice.

market (v.)
marketer (n.)

2. a. The various __________ of fruit must ship their produce in refrigerated trucks.
   b. They __________ a new type of apple next season.

consume (v.)
consumer (n.)

3. a. Enthusiastic __________ of fruit are very demanding. They want only the freshest fruit.
   b. They __________ tons of fruit every year.

employ (v.)
employer (n.)

4. a. When she began her own company, Ms. Harris __________ anyone who had very little experience.
   b. Like other __________, she wanted experienced people who didn't need much training.

work (v.)
worker (n.)

5. a. Mark is a very dependable __________.
   b. He always __________ hard and does his job well.

Part 2

In English, adjectives can change to verbs. Some adjectives become verbs by adding the suffix *-en,*—for example, *light* (adj.), becomes *lighten* (v.).

Complete each sentence with the correct form of the words on the left. **Use the correct tense of the verb in either the affirmative or the negative form.**

broad (adj.) broaden (v.)	1. a. Betty went to college to study French, but she felt that her major was not ________ enough. b. Next semester she ___________ her major to Romance languages, and study Spanish and Portuguese as well as French.
wide (adj.) widen (v.)	2. a. The government ________________ the old highway, although it is too narrow. b. Instead, the government is planning a new highway, which will be very ______________.
sweet (adj.) sweeten (v.)	3. a. Joseph loves to drink very _____________ coffee. b. He ________________ his coffee by adding four teaspoons of sugar to his cup.
short (adj.) shorten (v.)	4. a. The factory workers want a ____________ work week, so they had a demonstration at the factory. b. The company ______________ their work week from 45 to 40 hours a week next month.
long (adj.) lengthen (v.)	5. a. The American government ___________ some weekends because mid-week holidays are inconvenient. b. Now some holidays are celebrated on Monday, so everyone has a ____________ weekend.

• F. Vocabulary in Context

alert (adj.)
awareness (n.)
compile (v.)
favorite (adj.)
habit (n.)
nutritional (adj.)
rush (v.)
skip (v.)
survey (n.)
variety (n.)

Read the following sentences. Complete each blank space with the correct word from the list above. Use each word only once.

1. Children like a _______________ of food in their diet. For example, at breakfast they like to choose among cereal, pancakes, doughnuts, or eggs and toast.
2. If you do not understand one part of the test, you can _______________ to the next part and go back to the difficult part later.
3. Joan's train was scheduled to leave at 6 P.M. It was 5:50, so she had to _______________ in order not to miss her train.
4. Dean and Jenny are going to _______________ a list of all the places they want to visit on their next trip across the country.
5. I like all kinds of cake, cookies, and ice cream, but my _______________ dessert is chocolate ice cream. I like it best of all!
6. The college cafeteria manager is going to do a _______________ of the students to help her decide which foods students prefer.
7. Small children have very little _______________ of the dangers of running into the street.
8. Fruit and vegetables are an important part of a _______________ diet.
9. Many students drink large quantities of coffee to keep them _______________ while they are studying for an important exam.
10. Ann has a _______________ of smoking cigarettes with her morning coffee.

• G. Topics for Discussion and Writing

1. Are lifestyles also changing in your country? Why? Describe how they are changing. Are they similar to the lifestyles in the United States today?
2. In your country, do people eat differently today than they did in the past? Give reasons and examples in your explanation.
3. In your country, what do you eat in various situations (for example, to increase athletic ability, to lose weight, to be alert for business, for romance)? Why?
4. Describe your present lifestyle. What do you like about it? What do you dislike about it?

• H. Follow-Up Activities

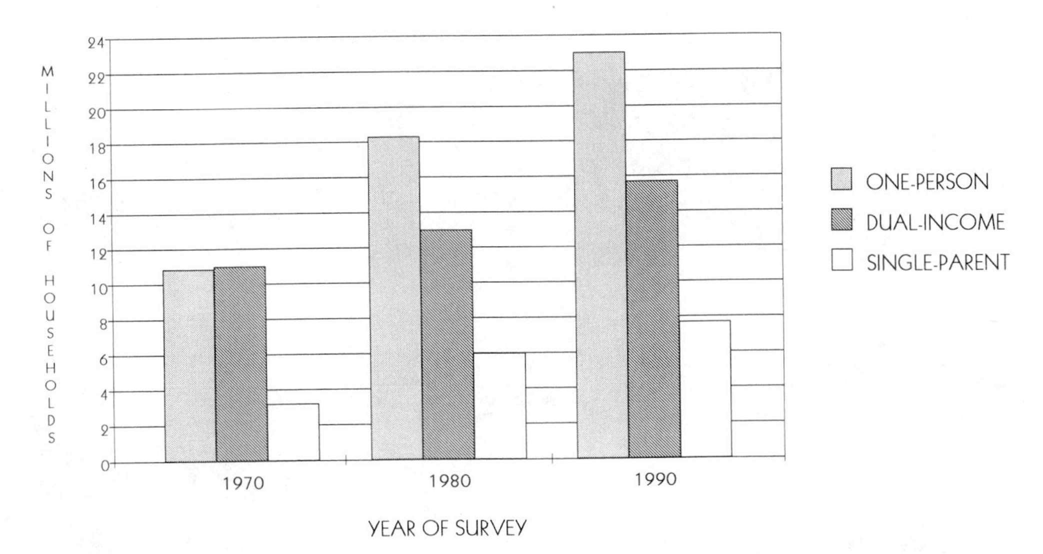

1. Refer to the bar graph. Read the following sentences, and fill in the blank spaces with the correct answer.

   a. There were ___________ million one-person households in the United States in 1970.
   b. There were __________ million dual-income households in the United States in 1980.
   c. There were __________ million single-parent households in the United States in 1990.
   d. From 1970 to 1990, the greatest percentage increase was in ___________ households.
   e. From 1970 to 1990, the smallest percentage increase was in ___________ households.

2. Many different factors can affect the way we eat. For example, if you are a very busy person, you may not have a lot of time for meals. As a result, you may not cook very much or you may eat out often. On the other hand, you may have a lot of free time. How would this affect your eating habits? Think about some different factors, list them below, and write about how they affect eating habits.

Factor	Effect on Eating Habits
1. time	
2. money	
3.	
4.	
5.	

C·H·A·P·T·E·R 3

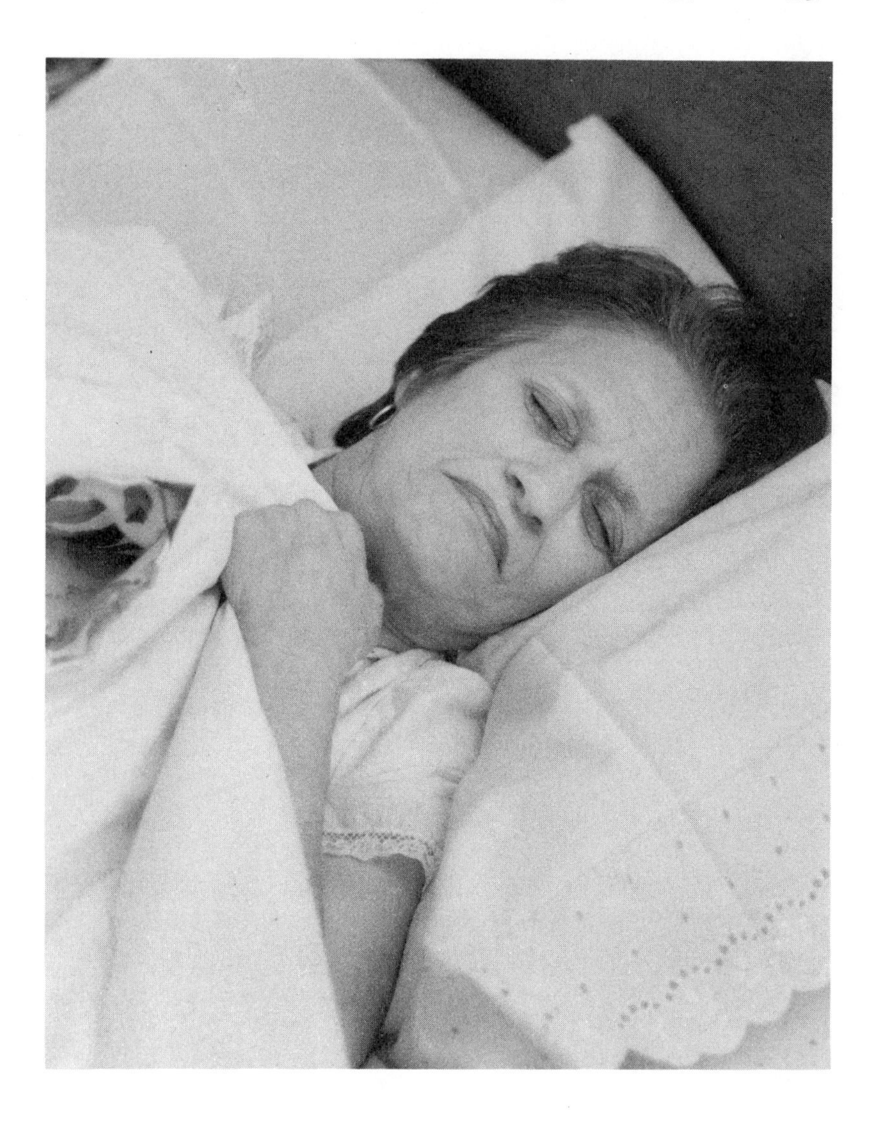

Dreams: Making Them Work for Us

• Prereading Preparation

1. What are dreams?
2. How often do you have dreams? Do you usually remember them?
3. Do you think dreams are important? Why or why not? Read the title of this article. What do you think it means?
4. Describe a dream you have had. Then work together with a classmate. Read about each other's dream. What do you think your classmate's dream means?

My Dream

____

____

____

____

5. Have you ever had a nightmare (a bad dream)? How did you feel after you woke up?

---

1 Several nights a week Joseph woke up screaming
2 from the same terrible dream. Joseph could never recall
3 his whole dream, though. He only remembered that
4 someone was running after him. Joseph was trying to
5 get away, but in his dream he could not move. He con-
6 tinued having this nightmare for months. He was so
7 tired in the morning that it was hard for him to go to
8 work. Joseph, you see, is not a frightened child, but a
9 grown man.
10 Milton Kramer is a psychiatrist and dream researcher
11 in Cincinnati, Ohio. He believes that it is very important
12 that people don't ignore their dreams, because they are

messages from our sleeping minds. When Kramer studied dreams and dreamers, he found that people wake up feeling very discouraged after they have a bad dream. He also found that after having a good dream, people feel more optimistic. Clearly, dreams can have harmful or beneficial effects. As a result, Kramer believes that we need to learn how to change our bad dreams. When we understand what happened in our dreams, we can change negative, hurtful dreams to positive, helpful ones.

Before we can begin to change a nightmare, however, we first have to remember what happened in our dream. Researchers say there are many ways to do this. We can keep a journal or diary of what we do when we are awake. Then, before going to sleep, we can review our day. This practice helps us connect our dreams with daily life. As we begin to fall asleep, we should remind ourselves that we want to remember our dreams. This reminder helps us to stay in charge. When we wake up, we should lie still while we try to remember our dream. Dream researchers say that by staying in the same sleeping position, we are more likely to recall the dream. We should also try to remember an important word or picture from the dream. This image makes the rest of the dream easier to remember. Finally, if we have trouble remembering dreams, we can try sleeping later. The longer we sleep, the longer and more complex our dreams will be.

Dr. Rosalind Cartwright is a dream researcher, too. She has developed another dream therapy for changing dreams. According to Dr. Cartwright, dream therapy involves four simple steps you can learn on your own. The first step is to recognize when you are having a bad dream that will make you feel helpless or upset the next morning. The second step is to identify what it is about the dream that makes you feel bad—for example, weak instead of strong, or out of control instead of in control. Next, stop any bad dream. You do not have to continue your bad dream, because you are in charge. The last step is to change the negative part of the dream. Sometimes you may have to wake yourself up and change the dream before you return to sleep. Other times it is possible to change the dream while you are still asleep.

56 By using dream therapy, Joseph was able to change
57 his nightmares. Gradually, his bad dreams stopped alto-
58 gether. He began having more positive dreams and woke
59 up feeling refreshed and cheerful. A night of good
60 dreaming can leave us all in a better mood in the morn-
61 ing. We feel well rested and more optimistic. Stopping a
62 nightmare and changing it to a positive dream experi-
63 ence can be physically and psychologically beneficial to
64 us all.

• A. Fact-Finding Exercise

Read the passage again. Read the following statements. Check whether they are True (T) or False (F). If a statement is false, rewrite the statement so that it is true. Then go back to the passage and find the line that supports your answer.

______ T ______ F 1. Joseph had the same bad dream for a long time.

____

______ T ______ F 2. Milton Kramer does not believe that dreams are important.

____

_____ T _____ F 3. Many people feel discouraged after they have a good dream.

____

_____ T _____ F 4. There are many ways to help us remember our dreams.

____

_____ T _____ F 5. Our dreams are usually shorter when we sleep a long time.

____

_____ T _____ F 6. Dream therapy can help us change our bad dreams.

____

_____ T _____ F 7. Joseph's bad dreams never stopped.

____

• B. Reading Analysis

Read each question carefully. Either circle the letter of the correct answer, or write your answer in the space provided.

1. What is the main idea of the passage?

   a. Joseph was finally able to change his nightmares by using dream therapy.
   b. Dreams are very important, and it is possible to change a bad dream into a good dream.
   c. Dream therapy has four simple steps for success.

2. Read lines 2–4. In these two sentences, which word is a synonym for **recall**?

   ____

3. In line 9, what is a **grown man**?

   a. an adult
   b. a frightened child
   c. a tall man

4. Read lines 13–22.

   a. What are **dreamers**?

      1. people who wake up after a dream
      2. people who dream
      3. people who study dreams

b. In these lines, what is the opposite (antonym) of **discouraged**?

1. harmful
2. beneficial
3. optimistic

c. What does **harmful** mean?

1. dangerous
2. discouraged
3. optimistic

d. In these lines, what is the opposite (antonym) of **harmful**?

1. discouraged
2. effects
3. beneficial

5. Read lines 23–29.

a. What does **this** refer to?

1. to change a nightmare
2. to remember our dreams
3. to keep a diary

b. What is a **journal**?

1. a dream
2. a diary
3. a review

c. What is **this practice**?

1. going to sleep
2. remembering our dreams
3. keeping a journal

6. Read lines 35–37. What is **this image**?

a. an important word or picture
b. the whole dream
c. the way we sleep

7. Read lines 41–44. "**According to** Dr. Cartwright" means

a. Dr. Cartwright said
b. Dr. Cartwright proved
c. Dr. Cartwright agreed

8. Read lines 44–52. Put the following dream therapy steps in the correct order.

   ______ Change the negative part of the dream.
   ______ Identify the part of the dream that makes you feel bad.
   ______ Recognize when you are having a bad dream.
   ______ Stop your bad dream.

9. Read lines 56–59.

   a. **Gradually** means

      1. quickly
      2. slowly
      3. carefully

   b. **Altogether** means

      1. completely
      2. suddenly
      3. gradually

• C. Information Organization

Read the passage again. Underline what you think are the main ideas. Then scan the reading and complete the following chart, using the sentences that you have underlined to help you. You will use this chart later to answer questions about the reading.

How To Remember and Change Dreams	
Ways to Remember a Dream	How to Change a Dream: - Dream Therapy -
1. During the day: a. b. c. As you fall asleep:	1.
2. When you wake up: a. b.	2. When you wake up: a. b.
3. If you have trouble remembering your dreams:	3. To stop any bad dream:
	4. Change the negative part of the dream: a. b.

• D. Information Recall and Summary

Read each question carefully. Use your chart to answer the questions. Do not refer back to the passage. When you are finished, write a brief summary of the reading.

1. How can we help ourselves remember a dream *before* we go to sleep?

2. How can we help ourselves remember a dream after we wake up?

3. What can we do if we can't remember our dreams?

4. Describe the four steps in dream therapy.

Summary

Work in pairs or alone. Write a brief summary of the reading, and put it on the blackboard. Compare your summary with your classmates'. Which one best describes the main idea of the reading?

• E. Word Forms

Part 1

In English, verbs change to adjectives in several ways. Some verbs become adjectives by adding the suffix *-ful*—for example, *doubt* (v.), becomes *doubtful* (adj.).

Complete each sentence with the correct form of the words on the left. **Use the correct tense of the verb in either the affirmative or the negative form.**

cheer (v.) cheerful (adj.)	1. a. When Rachel was in the hospital, her friends visited her and __________ her up. b. She felt very __________ after their visits.
help (v.) helpful (adj.)	2. a. Curt had a headache, so he took some aspirin, but they __________. His headache didn't go away. b. Because the aspirin weren't __________, Curt had to leave work early.
rest (v.) restful (adj.)	3. a. Next month, Henry is going on vacation. He __________ for two weeks. b. His job is quite stressful, so he needs a __________ vacation this year.
use (v.) useful (adj.)	4. a. Maureen always __________ a typewriter to do her schoolwork when she was in high school. She didn't like computers. b. When she entered college, she learned how to use a computer and realized just how __________ it really was.
harm (v.) harmful (adj.)	5. a. Most people know that cigarettes are very __________ to a smoker's health. b. However, cigarette smoke can also __________ the health of people who live with smokers.

Part 2

In English, some adjectives have two forms, depending on their meaning. Some adjectives have an *-ed* form and an *-ing* form—for example, *excited* and *exciting*.

Complete each sentence with the correct adjective form of the words on the left.

frightened (adj.) frightening (adj.)	1. a. Craig saw a very __________ movie last Saturday. b. He was so __________ that his friends walked home with him.
tired (adj.) tiring (adj.)	2. a. Standing all day at work is a __________ experience. b. Many people become __________ just from standing on a hard floor.
discouraged (adj.) discouraging (adj.)	3. a. The teacher gave his students a very difficult math test. The results of the test were very __________ because none of the students did well. b. The teacher was very __________, but he reviewed the math with the class and gave another test. This time the students' grades were much better.
refreshed (adj.) refreshing (adj.)	4. a. During the summer, Gloria swims in her pool every afternoon because it's so __________. b. She always feels cool and __________ after her afternoon swim.
interested (adj.) interesting (adj.)	5. a. The class is quite __________ in going to the Natural History Museum. b. The museum has an extremely __________ exhibit on tropical rain forests that the students want to see.

• F. Vocabulary in Context

Read the following sentences. Complete each blank space with the correct word from the list above. Use each word only once.

altogether (adv.)	gradually (adv.)	journal (n.)
cheerful (adj.)	grown (adj.)	practice (n.)
discouraged (adj.)	harmful (adj.)	recall (v.)
dream (v.)		

1. I have met Trudy's brother several times, but I can't __________ his name.

2. Janet keeps her __________ on her computer. She has written in it regularly for several years.

3. Olga wanted to improve her typing speed, so she practiced every day. __________ she became a skilled typist.

4. Simon is a very __________ person. He always seems happy and optimistic.

5. The teacher has a useful __________ of writing our homework on the blackboard every day.

6. I almost always __________ when I've had a busy day.

7. Many children are afraid of the dark, but by the time they are __________, they have overcome their fear.

8. William wanted to stop drinking coffee, so every week he drank fewer cups. For one week, he drank eight cups a day. Then he drank four cups a day for another week. After four weeks, he was able to stop drinking coffee __________.

9. Over a long period of time, not getting enough sleep may be __________ to your health.

10. Jason feels __________ about learning Russian. He studied for his Russian test, but he still didn't do well.

• G. Topics For Discussion And Writing

1. Read the last paragraph of the article again. Write about Joseph's nightmares. How do you think he changed them?
2. In many cultures, certain themes in dreams have specific meanings. For example, in the United States, a dream about falling usually means that we feel helpless or out of control. Flying generally means that we feel successful and satisfied with ourselves. Being chased in a dream often signifies a danger from other people. In your culture, do falling, flying, and being chased have the same meaning, or different ones? Think about how your culture interprets dreams. Discuss this and give examples.

• H. Follow-Up Activity

Refer back to the chart in Exercise C. Review the four steps in changing a dream. Use the chart below, and begin with the first step: Briefly describe a bad dream that you recently had. Work with a partner. Together, read about each other's dream. Then discuss the other three steps, and help each other identify the negative parts of your dreams and develop strategies for stopping a bad dream and for changing a bad dream. Compare your strategies with your classmates'.

How To Change a Dream: – Dream Therapy –	
Describe a recent bad dream.	
Identify what it was about the dream that made you feel bad.	
Strategies for stopping a bad dream.	
Strategies for changing the negative part of the dream.	

Unit I Review

• I. Crossword Puzzle

Clues

Across

4. happy; in a good mood
6. I usually ___ my coffee with two teaspoons of sugar
8. An adult is a ___ person.
11. slowly; little by little
14. impolite
16. diary
17. the opposite of *down*
20. amount
22. It is a bad idea to ___ breakfast. You should eat breakfast every morning.
24. bad dream
26. John give me this job. He is my _____.
28. actions
30. If I hurt someone's feelings, I always ___. I always say that I am sorry.

Down

1. completely
2. remember
3. ___, two, three
5. hurtful; detrimental
7. picture
9. although
10. however
12. John feels very ___. He keeps trying to learn English, but he hasn't been successful.
13. People in a new country need to ___, or change, to the different customs.
15. A good ___ reads labels and buys products carefully.
18. status; rank
19. way of living
21. alert
23. I wanted to go to the movies, but I stayed home and studied ___.
25. Farmers ___ wheat, corn, rice, and other grains.
27. We ___ learning English.
29. I come ___ class on time every day.

• J. Unit I Discussion

1. The three chapters in this unit discuss trends in living in the American culture: being on time, changing lifestyles, eating habits, and dreams. Work in a group of three or four and discuss the following questions.

   a. How do these features describe American culture as a whole? What do you think is important to Americans?
   b. Select one of these aspects of American life, and compare it with your own or another culture. How is it similar? How is it different?

2. Think about these features (being on time, changing lifestyles, eating habits, and dreams) in your own culture. Do people in your country feel the same about these features as Americans do? What would you say is important to the people in your culture?

Unit II

Issues in Society

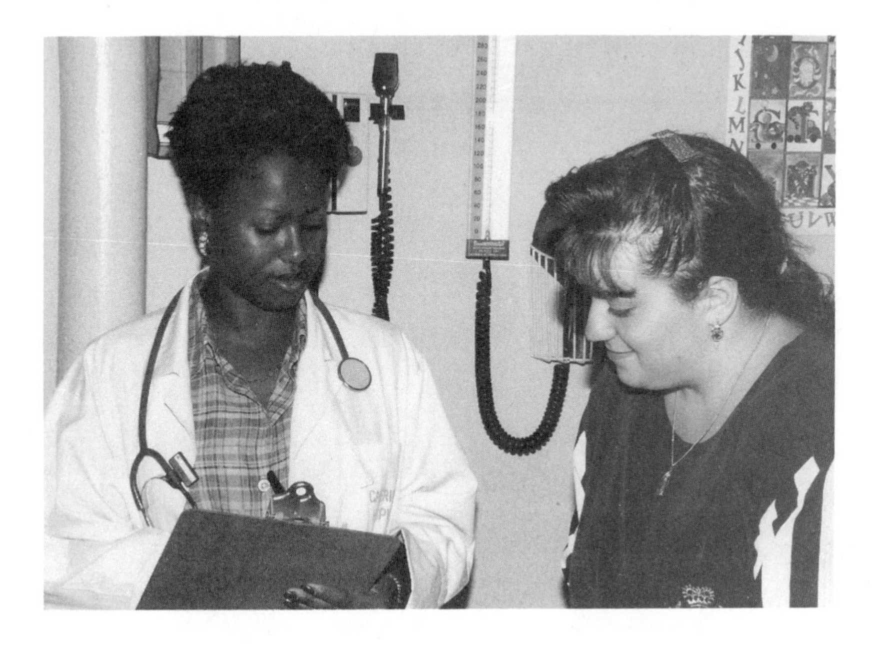

CHAPTER 4

AMERICAN SIGN LANGUAGE (ASL)

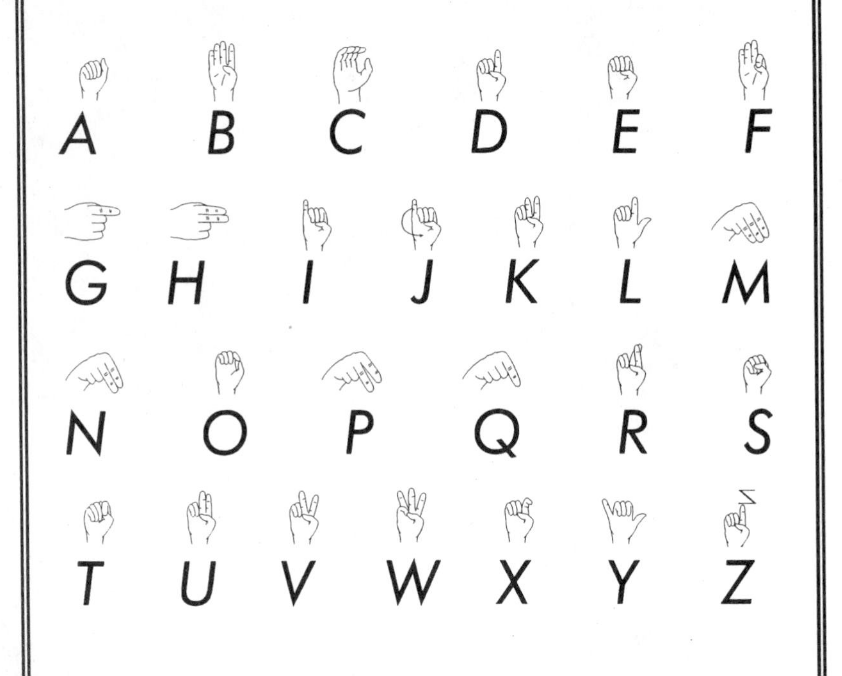

Language: Is It Always Spoken?

• Prereading Preparation

1. What is language?
   a. Work with two partners and write a definition of the word **language** in the box below.
   b. Write your group's definition of **language** on the blackboard. Compare your definition with your classmates' definitions.
   c. Look up the word **language** in your dictionary, and compare it to your definition.

Your Group's Definition	The Dictionary Definition

2. At what age do most babies learn to speak? How do they learn to speak?
3. How do you think deaf babies learn to communicate?
4. How do deaf people communicate?
5. Look at the American Manual Alphabet on page 46. Who uses it and why?
   a. In groups of three, use the sign language chart to learn to "sign" an object in the room—for example, **chair** or **pen.**
   b. Demonstrate your word to your classmates, and they will give the name of the object.
6. Read the title of this passage. Reread your definitions of **language.** Do you think human language must be spoken? Is there any other way that people can communicate?

Most of us know a little about how babies learn to talk. From the time infants are born, they hear language because their parents talk to them all the time. Between the ages of seven and ten months, most infants begin to make sounds. They repeat the same sounds over and over again. For example, a baby may repeat the sound "dadada" or "bababa." This activity is called babbling. When babies babble, they are practicing their language. Soon, the sound "dadada" may become "daddy," and "bababa" may become "bottle."

What happens, though, to children who cannot hear? How do deaf children learn to communicate? Recently, doctors have learned that deaf babies babble with their hands. Laura Ann Petitto, a psychologist at McGill University in Montreal, Canada, has studied how children learn language. She observed three hearing infants and two deaf infants. The three hearing infants had English-speaking parents. The two deaf infants had deaf mothers and fathers who used American Sign Language (ASL) to communicate with each other and with their babies. Dr. Petitto studied the babies three times: at 10, 12, and 14 months. During this time, children really begin to develop their language skills.

After watching and videotaping the children for several hundred hours, the psychologist and her assistants made many important observations. For example, they saw that the hearing children made many different, varied motions with their hands. However, there appeared to be no pattern to these motions. The deaf babies also made many different movements with their hands, but these movements were more consistent and deliberate. The deaf babies seemed to make the same hand movements over and over again. During the four-month period, the deaf babies' hand motions started to resemble some of the basic hand-shapes used in ASL. The children also seemed to prefer certain hand-shapes.

Hearing infants start first with simple syllable babbling (dadada), then put more syllables together to sound like real sentences and questions. Apparently, deaf babies follow this same pattern, too. First, they repeat simple hand-shapes. Next, they form some simple hand signs (words) and use these movements together to resemble ASL sentences.

Linguists—people who study language—believe that our ability for language is innate. In other words, humans are born with the capacity for language. It does not matter if we are physically able to speak or not. Language can be expressed in many different ways—for instance, by speech or by sign. Dr. Petitto believes this theory and wants to prove it. She plans to study hearing children who have one deaf parent and one hearing parent. Dr. Petitto wants to see what happens when babies have the opportunity to learn both sign language and speech. Does the human brain prefer speech? Some of these studies of hearing babies who have one deaf parent and one hearing parent show that the babies babble equally with their hands and their voices. They also produce their first words, both spoken and signed, at about the same time.

The capacity for language is uniquely human. More studies in the future may prove that the sign system of the deaf is the physical equivalent of speech. If so, the old theory that only the spoken word is language will have to be changed. The whole concept of human communication will have a very new and different meaning.

• A. Fact-Finding Exercise

Read the passage again. Read the following statements. Check whether they are True (T) or False (F). If a statement is false, rewrite the statement so that it is true. Then go back to the passage and find the line that supports your answer.

_____ T _____ F 1. Most infants start to babble before they are a year old.

____

_____ T _____ F 2. Dr. Petitto studied only deaf babies.

____

_____ T _____ F 3. The psychologist saw that deaf babies and hearing babies moved their hands the same way.

____

_____ T _____ F 4. Dr. Petitto believes that we are all born with the ability for language.

____

_____ T _____ F 5. Dr. Petitto believes that hearing babies who have one deaf parent and one hearing parent produce their first spoken words before their first signed words.

____

B. Reading Analysis

Read each question carefully, Either circle the letter of the correct answer, or write your answer in the space provided.

1. What is the main idea of the passage?

   a. Both deaf children and hearing children learn to communicate in similar ways at about the same time.
   b. Children begin to develop their language skills at around two years of age.
   c. Many linguists believe that all humans are born with the ability to speak.

2. Read lines 5–7. What is **babbling**?

   ____

3. Read lines 18–20.

   a. What is **ASL**?

   ____

   b. Who uses ASL? Why?

   ____

4. Read lines 24–28. What is an **observation**?

   a. something you see or hear
   b. something you write
   c. something important

5. In lines 27–28, what are **varied motions**?

   a. different sounds
   b. different movements
   c. different signs

6. Read lines 26–33: "They saw that the hearing children made many different, varied motions with their hands. However, there appeared to be no pattern to these motions. The deaf babies also made many different movements with their hands, but these movements were more consistent and deliberate. The deaf babies seemed to make the same hand movements over and over again."

   a. Which of the following statements are true?

      1. All children make motions with their hands.
      2. Only the deaf children made many different movements with their hands.
      3. The hearing children's hand movements had a pattern.
      4. The deaf children's hand movements had a pattern.

   b. Complete the following sentence correctly.
   Both the deaf and the hearing children made movements with their hands, but

      1. only the hearing children made different movements
      2. they all made the same movements over and over again
      3. only the deaf children repeated the same hand motions
      4. only the hearing children repeated the same hand motions

7. Read lines 33–36: "During the four-month period, the deaf babies' hand motions started to resemble some of the basic hand-shapes used in ASL." This sentence means that

   a. the deaf babies were studying ASL.
   b. the deaf babies were repeating their parents' hand signs.
   c. the deaf babies stopped babbling.

8. Read lines 44—46: "Linguists—people who study language—believe that our ability for language is innate. In other words, humans are born with the capacity for language."

   a. What is a **linguist**?

   ____

   b. How do you know?

   ____

   c. What does **capacity** mean?

      1. language
      2. ability
      3. belief

   d. What does **innate** mean?

      1. something you are born with
      2. something you are able to do
      3. something a linguist believes

   e. What follows **in other words**?

      1. a new idea
      2. an explanation of the previous idea
      3. an example of the previous idea

9. a. In lines 47–49, what are some different ways we can express language?

   ____

   b. What does **for instance** mean?

      1. however
      2. so that
      3. for example

10. Read lines 60–64.

    If so means
    a. if everyone agrees
    b. if this is true

• C. Information Organization

Read the passage again. Underline what you think are the main ideas. Then scan the reading and complete the following outline, using the sentences that you have underlined to help you. You will use this outline later to answer questions about the reading.

I. How Babies Learn Language

A. Hearing Babies

1.

2.

B.

1.

2.

II.

A. Who Conducted the Experiment:

B. Who She Studied:

C. How She Studied Them:

D. Conclusion:

III. Future Experiments

A. Theory:

B. Who She Will Study:

C. Purpose of the Experiment:

• D. Information Recall and Summary

Read each question carefully. Use your outline to answer the questions. Do not refer back to the passage. When you are finished, write a brief summary of the reading.

1. a. What is babbling?

   ____

   b. When does it occur?

   ____

2. Who did Dr. Petitto study? Why?

   ____

3. What did the psychologist and her assistants discover after they watched the videotapes of the children?

   ____

4. What theory does Dr. Petitto believe about language learning?

   ____

5. Who does this psychologist want to study next? Why?

   ____

Summary

Work in pairs or alone. Write a brief summary of the reading, and put it on the blackboard. Compare your summary with your classmates'. Which one best describes the main idea of the reading?

____

____

____

____

• E. Word Forms

Part 1

In English, verbs change to nouns in several ways. Some verbs become nouns by adding the suffix *-ing*—for example, *learn* (v.), becomes *learning* (n.).

Complete each sentence with the correct form of the words on the left. **Use the correct tense of the verb in either the affirmative or the negative form. Use the singular or plural form of the noun.**

talk (v.) talking (n.)	1. a. For most people, __________ is an important social activity. b. Unfortunately, some people __________ too much.
begin (v.) beginning (n.)	2. a. Harry needs to rewrite his composition. He __________ each paragraph with an indentation, but he should have. b. A composition needs an indentation at the __________ of every paragraph.
hear (v.) hearing (n.)	3. a. The school nurse checks the __________ of all the students in every class. b. If a child __________ well, the nurse informs the parents and suggests that they take their child to a doctor.
babble (v.) babbling (n.)	4. a. Rod and Cheryl's baby __________ all the time. b. They are very excited about her __________ because she is saying "mama" and "dada."
mean (v.) meaning (n.)	5. a. The verb *get* __________ so many different things that I sometimes have trouble understanding it in a sentence. b. The word *get* has so many different __________ that I become confused.

Part 2

In English, adjectives change to nouns in several ways. Some adjectives become nouns by changing the final *-t* to *-ce*—for example, *ignorant* (adj.), becomes *ignorance* (n.).

Complete each sentence with the correct form of the words on the left. **Use the singular or plural form of the noun.**

important (adj.) importance (n.)	1. a. Whether you write a composition with a pen or pencil is of very little __________. b. What is much more __________ is the content of the composition.
different (adj.) difference (n.)	2. a. Some languages aren't very __________ from each other—for example, Spanish and Portuguese. b. Other languages, however, have significant __________—for example, Chinese and French.
significant (adj.) significance (n.)	3. a. The introduction of the personal computer several years ago had ________ effects on our everyday lives. b. We can understand the unbelievable __________ of this machine when we realize that today there are tens of millions of PCs in the United States alone.
dependent (adj.) dependence (n.)	4. a. As children grow up, their __________ on their parents decreases. b. However, children usually remain financially __________ on their parents for many years.
persistent (adj.) persistence (n.)	5. a. Rebecca is an incredibly __________ person. She studied hard for four years to get a scholarship to college. b. As a result of her __________, she did well on her tests and got a scholarship to a good university.

• F. Vocabulary in Context

Read the following sentences. Complete each blank space with the correct word or phrase from the list above. Use each word or phrase only once.

capacity (n.)	in other words	observation (n.)
for instance	meaning (n.)	persistent (adj.)
if so	motion (n.)	varied (adj.)
innate (adj.)		

1. Eugene is a very __________ student. He never stops working until he finishes a job, regardless of how difficult it is for him.

2. It may rain on Saturday. __________, we won't go on a picnic. We'll see a movie instead.

3. If Jackie doesn't understand the __________ of a word from the context, she uses her English dictionary.

4. Animals do not have the __________ for speech. Only humans can communicate with language.

5. Henry has a __________ life. During the day, he is a student. In the evenings, he works as a waiter. On Saturdays, he teaches swimming to children, and on Sundays, he sings in a choir.

6. Researchers have to have training in __________. They need to learn what to look for and how to record what they see.

7. Human babies have many __________ abilities. Walking and speaking are two of them.

8. In different cultures, the same __________, such as waving your hand, may have different meanings.

9. Janet complains about everything, from the food to the trains. She's always too warm or too cold. She doesn't like anything. __________, Janet is a very negative person.

10. Mathew enjoys going out to restaurants to experience eating the food of different cultures. __________, one month he will go to an Indian restaurant. Then he will try Japanese food. After that, he will go to a Colombian or a Greek restaurant.

• G. Topics for Discussion and Writing

1. Many famous people of the past and present have been deaf. Despite their disability, they were successful in their lives. For example, Helen Keller was an important author and scholar, and Marlee Matlin is a famous American actress. What other famous people do you know who were or are hearing-impaired (deaf)? Write about one of these people. Tell about what that person has accomplished in spite of his or her disability.
2. Sign language is one important form of nonverbal communication. Can you think of another type of nonverbal communication? Describe it.

• H. Follow-Up Activities

1. Doctors have developed a controversial operation (a cochlear implant) to enable the deaf to "hear." Many deaf people are opposed to this operation. They say that they are not really disabled. They feel they are a minority group and should be accepted as they are—nonhearing people. They feel it is wrong to force children to have this operation and that the operation does not really enable the deaf to hear as well as nondeaf people do anyway. They feel that their sign language should be accepted as any spoken language is.

   Work in a group of four. Make a list of the advantages and disadvantages of remaining deaf (and not having the operation) and the advantages and disadvantages of having the operation. Next to your list of advantages and disadvantages, write the consequences of remaining deaf and the consequences of being able to "hear." Compare your list with your classmates' lists.

2. Many deaf people feel that ASL is a real language. They believe that hearing people should learn it, just as they learn other languages. The American Manual Alphabet on page 46 is only for "spelling" out words, letter by letter. Go to the library and find a book on learning ASL. In small groups, learn to "sign" some basic rules and sentences. Then, in your group, discuss what it may be like to learn ASL, compared to learning a spoken language. Discuss your conclusions with your classmates.

C·H·A·P·T·E·R 5

Loneliness: How Can We Overcome It?

• Prereading Preparation

1. What is **loneliness**?

2. Are **loneliness** and being **alone** the same? Why or why not?

3. Look at the table below. Work with a partner and make a list of some reasons why people may feel lonely. Have you or your partner ever felt lonely for these reasons? Discuss your answers with your classmate.

Reasons People Feel Lonely	You	Your Partner
1.	yes/no	yes/no
2.	yes/no	yes/no
3.	yes/no	yes/no
4.	yes/no	yes/no
5.	yes/no	yes/no

4. Do you think everyone feels lonely at some time in his or her life? Do you think this is common? Explain your answer.

5. How would you answer the question in the title of this chapter?

Most people feel lonely sometimes, but it usually only lasts between a few minutes and a few hours. This kind of loneliness is not serious. In fact, it is quite normal. For some people, though, loneliness can last for years. Psychologists are studying this complex phenomenon in an attempt to better understand long-term loneliness. These researchers have already identified three different types of loneliness.

The first kind of loneliness is temporary. This is the most common type. It usually disappears quickly and does not require any special attention. The second kind, situational loneliness, is a natural result of a particular situation—for example, a divorce, the death of a loved one, or moving to a new place. Although this kind of loneliness can cause physical problems, such as headaches and sleeplessness, it usually does not last for more than a year. Situational loneliness is easy to understand and to predict.

The third kind of loneliness is the most severe. Unlike the second type, chronic loneliness usually lasts more than two years and has no specific cause. People who experience habitual loneliness have problems socializing and becoming close to others. Unfortunately, many chronically lonely people think there is little or nothing they can do to improve their condition.

Psychologists agree that one important factor in loneliness is a person's social contacts, e.g., friends, family members, coworkers, etc. We depend on various people for different reasons. For instance, our families give us emotional support, our parents and teachers give us guidance, and our friends share similar interests and activities. However, psychologists have found that the number of social contacts we have is not the only reason for loneliness. It is more important how many social contacts we think or expect we should have. In other words, though lonely people may have many social contacts, they sometimes feel they should have more. They question their own popularity.

Most researchers agree that the loneliest people are between the ages of 18 and 25, so a group of psychologists decided to study a group of college freshmen. They found that more than 50% of the freshmen were situationally lonely at the beginning of the semester as a result of their new circumstances, but had adjusted after a few months. Thirteen percent were still lonely after seven months due to shyness and fear. They felt very uncomfortable meeting new people, even though they understood that their fear was not rational. The situationally lonely freshmen overcame their loneliness by making new friends, but the chronically lonely remained unhappy because they were afraid to do so.

Psychologists are trying to find ways to help habitually lonely people for two reasons. First of all, they are unhappy and unable to socialize. Secondly, researchers have found a connection between chronic loneliness and serious illnesses such as heart disease. While temporary and situational loneliness can be a normal, healthy part of life, chronic loneliness can be a very sad, and sometimes dangerous, condition.

• A. Fact-Finding Exercise

Read the passage again. Read the following statements. Check whether they are True (T) or False (F). If a statement is false, rewrite the statement so that it is true. Then go back to the passage and find the line that supports your answer.

_____ T _____ F 1. Psychologists say there are two different kinds of loneliness.

____

_____ T _____ F 2. All kinds of loneliness last only a short time.

____

_____ T _____ F 3. Temporary loneliness is very serious.

____

_____ T _____ F 4. Divorce sometimes causes loneliness.

____

_____ T _____ F 5. Loneliness can cause sleeplessness and headaches.

____

_____ T _____ F 6. Chronic loneliness usually lasts more than two years.

____

_____ T _____ F 7. Lonely people have no social contacts.

____

_____ T _____ F 8. The loneliest people are over 50 years old.

____

_____ T _____ F 9. Chronic loneliness can cause serious illness.

____

• B. Reading Analysis

Read each question carefully. Either circle the letter of the correct answer, or write your answer in the space provided.

1. What is the main idea of the passage?

   a. There are three different kinds of loneliness.
   b. Chronic loneliness is the most severe kind.
   c. Researchers want to cure loneliness.

2. Read lines 3–7.

   a. What does **last** mean?

      1. finish
      2. hurt
      3. continue

   b. What does **this complex phenomenon** refer to?

      1. loneliness that lasts for years
      2. loneliness that lasts for hours

3. Read lines 19–23.

   a. What does **unlike** show?

      1. a similarity
      2. a difference
      3. an addition

   b. Which word in these sentences is a synonym for **chronic**?

      ____

4. Read lines 26–28.

   a. What follows **e.g.**?

      1. examples
      2. proof
      3. explanations

   b. What does **etc.** mean?

      1. for example
      2. and others
      3. end of sentence

5. In line 29, **for instance** introduces

   a. explanations
   b. examples
   c. results

6. Read lines 34–38. How does **in other words** help you?

   ____

   ____

7. In line 38, what does **question** mean?

   a. ask a question
   b. have doubts about

8. Read lines 48–51.

   a. What does "the situationally lonely freshmen overcame their loneliness . . ." mean?

      1. They accepted their loneliness.
      2. They were no longer lonely.
      3. They made new friends.

   b. What does " . . .they were afraid to do so" mean?

   ____

9. Read lines 56–59. What does **while** mean?

   a. at the same time
   b. during
   c. although

• C. Information Organization

Read the passage again. Underline what you think are the main ideas. Then scan the reading and complete the following flowchart, using the sentences that you have underlined to help you. You will use this flowchart later to answer questions about the reading.

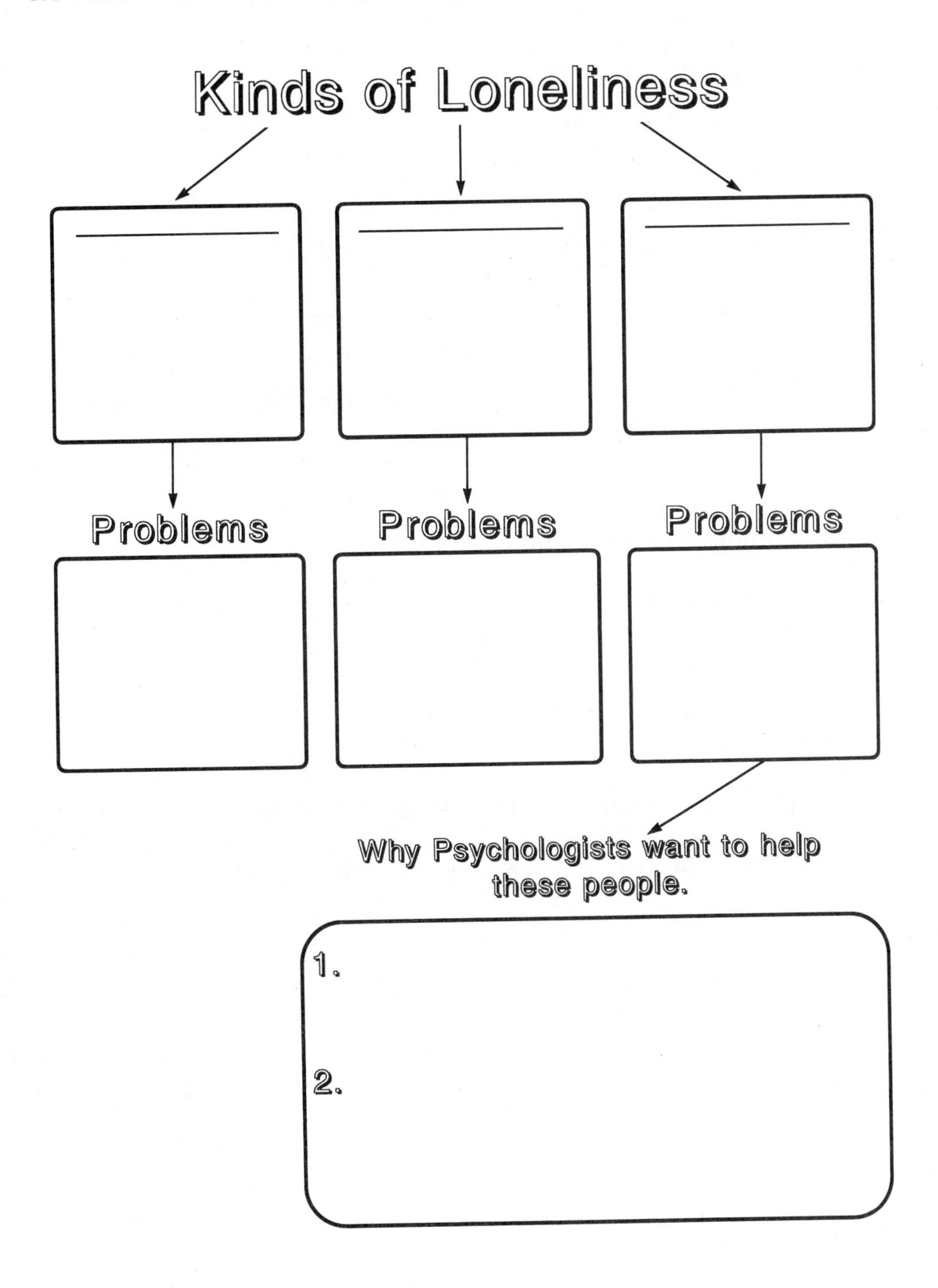

• D. Information Recall and Summary

Read each question carefully. Use your flowchart to answer the questions. Do not refer back to the passage. When you are finished, write a brief summary of the reading.

1. a. How many different kinds of loneliness are there?

   ____

   b. Describe each kind of loneliness.

   ____

   ____

   ____

2. Why is situational loneliness easy to predict?

   ____

   ____

3. Why is chronic loneliness the most severe kind of loneliness?

   ____

   ____

4. How can loneliness be unhealthy?

   ____

   ____

   ____

Summary

Work in pairs or alone. Write a brief summary of the reading, and put it on the blackboard. Compare your summary with your classmates'. Which one best describes the main idea of the reading?

____

____

____

____

____

• E. Word Forms

Part 1

In English, adjectives become nouns in several ways. Some adjectives become nouns by adding the suffix *-ness*—for example *sick* (adj.) becomes *sickness* (n.).

Complete each sentence with the correct form of the words on the left. **Use the singular or plural form of the noun.**

happy (adj.)
happiness (n.)

1. a. My nieces are very ___________ children.
   b. Their ___________ is important to my sister.

ill (adj.)
illness (n.)

2. a. The teacher left school early because she felt ___________ during class.
   b. Fortunately, her ___________ seemed to improve by the next morning.

lonely (adj.)
loneliness (n.)

3. a. My aunt overcame her ___________ by going out more often with her friends.
   b. She was very ___________ after her husband died.

shy (adj.)
shyness (n.)

4. a. Some doctors think that ___________ children are born that way.
   b. This ___________ often prevents them from doing well in school.

sleepless (adj.)
sleeplessness (n.)

5. a. My father finally went to the doctor because his ___________ was so severe.
   b. After several ___________ nights, he was exhausted.

Part 2

In English, some adjectives become nouns by adding the suffix *-ity*—for example, *national* (adj.) becomes *nationality* (n.).

Complete each sentence with the correct form of the words on the left. **Use the singular or plural form of the noun.**

complex (adj.)
complexity (n.)

1. a. The ________ of math depends on the type of math. For example, arithmetic is very simple.
   b. In contrast, calculus is a very ________ subject.

popular (adj.)
popularity (n.)

2. a. One of the most ________ fast foods in the United States is the hamburger.
   b. Its incredible ________ will probably continue for many years.

similar (adj.)
similarity (n.)

3. a. England and the United States are ________ because the people speak the same language.
   b. However, culturally, there are fewer ________ and many differences.

rational (adj.)
rationality (n.)

4. a. Under ordinary circumstances, most people act in a ________ manner.
   b. Under unusual circumstances, however, many people's level of ________ decreases.

equal (adj.)
equality (n.)

5. a. The American Constitution guarantees ________ to everyone under the law.
   b. In other words, every person living in the United States has ________ rights.

• F. Vocabulary in Context

chronic (adj.)
factors (n.)
for instance
overcame (v.)
predicted (v.)
remain (v.)
severe (adj.)
shy (adj.)
temporary (adj.)
unlike (adj.)

Read the following sentences. Complete each blank space with the correct word or phrase from the list above. Use each word or phrase only once.

1. Helen is very thin, ______________ her sister, who is quite heavy.
2. After I learn English, I will ___________ in this country and get a good job.
3. This beautiful weather is only __________. It is going to rain for the rest of this week.
4. Artie finally ________________ his fear of flying when he went to Florida by plane.
5. I am always waiting for Debbie because she is late for everything. Her ______________ lateness is destroying our friendship.
6. Yolanda is a _____________ student. She is very quiet and always sits alone in class.
7. This morning, the newscaster _____________ snow for tomorrow.
8. My uncle went to the hospital because he suddenly had a ________________ pain in his back.
9. A proper diet and frequent exercise are important _____________ in maintaining good health.
10. Barbara has many varied interests. ______________________, she enjoys music, horseback riding, and coin collecting.

• G. Topics for Discussion and Writing

1. Describe a time in your life when you felt lonely. What did you do to overcome your loneliness?
2. In this article, the author states that young adults (18 to 25 years old) are the loneliest people in the United States. Think about this statement. What do you think may be some reasons for this?
3. Do you think it is important for psychologists and researchers to study loneliness? Why or why not?

• H. Follow-Up Activity

In the article, the author states that in the United States, the loneliest people are young adults (18 to 25 years old). Is this also true in your country? Are different people lonely in different cultures? Take a survey in your class. Ask your classmates who the loneliest people are in their cultures. Then put the results of the survey on the blackboard. With your classmates, discuss what you think are the reasons for these results.

Country	Loneliest Age	Possible Reasons
U.S.A.	18–25	Many young people are in college and away from home.

C·H·A·P·T·E·R 6

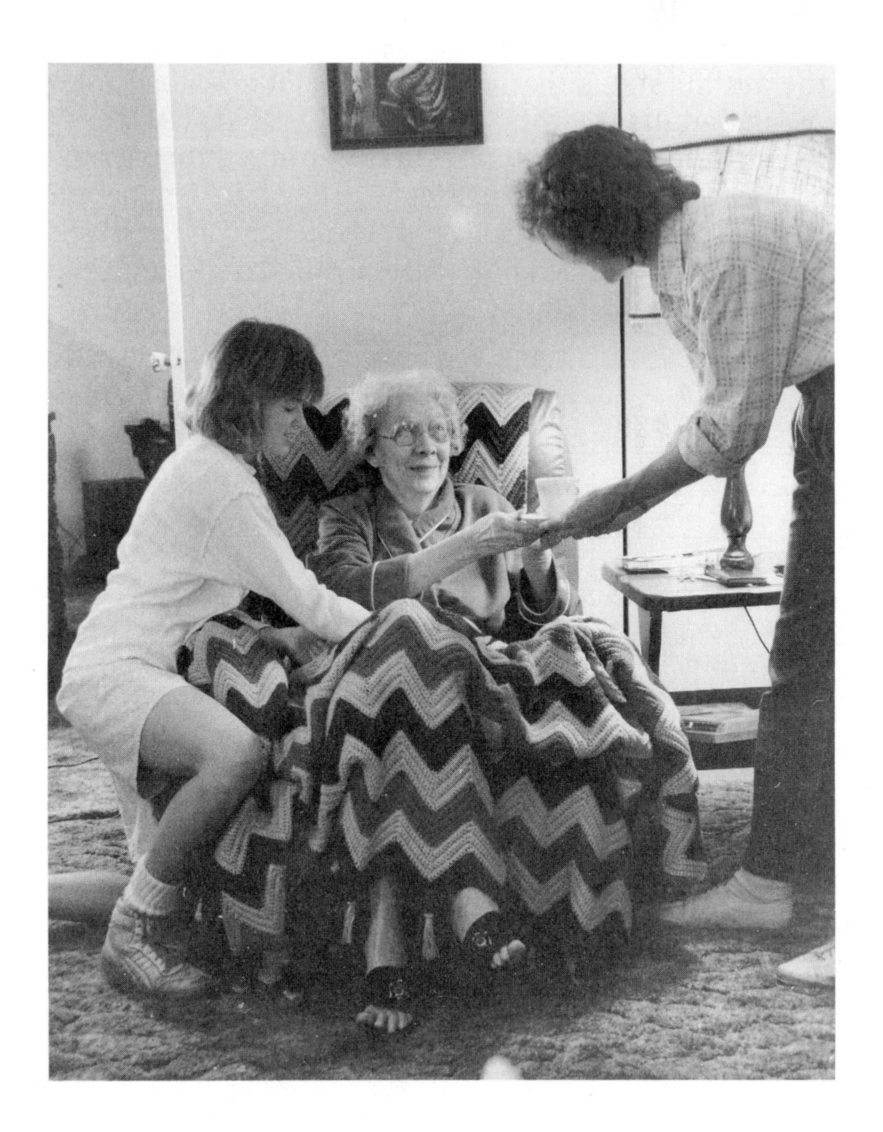

Care of the Elderly: A Family Matter

• Prereading Preparation

1. Who are the **elderly**?

2. a. What do you think happens to elderly people in the United States?

   b. Who do you think takes care of them?

   c. What gave you these ideas?

3. What is a **family matter**?

4. Read the title of this article. What do you think you are going to read about?

1 Who takes care of the elderly in the United States to-
2 day? The fact is that family members provide over 80%
3 of the care that elderly people need. Most times, the eld-
4 erly live in their own homes. A very small percent of
5 America's elderly live in nursing homes.
6 Samuel H. Preston, a sociologist at the University of
7 Pennsylvania, studied how the American family is
8 changing. He reported that by the time the average
9 American couple reaches 40 years of age, their parents
10 are usually still alive. This statistic shows the change in
11 lifestyles and responsibilities of aging Americans. The
12 average middle-aged couple can look forward to caring
13 for elderly parents sometime after their own children
14 have grown up. Moreover, because people today live
15 longer after an illness than people did years ago, family
16 members must provide long-term care. These facts also
17 mean that after caregivers provide for their elderly par-
18 ents, who will eventually die, they will be old and may

require care too. When they do, their spouses will probably take care of them because they have had fewer children than their parents did.

Because Americans are living longer than ever, more psychologists and social workers have begun to study ways of caregiving to improve care of the elderly. They have found that all caregivers share a common characteristic: They believe that they are the best person for the job, for different reasons. One caregiver said that she had always been close to her mother. Another was the oldest child. Another was the youngest child. Regardless of the reason, the caregivers all felt that they could do the job better than anyone else. Social workers interviewed caregivers to find out why they took on the responsibility of caring for an elderly, dependent relative. They discovered three basic reasons. Many caregivers believed that they had an obligation to help their relative. Some stated that helping others made them feel more useful. Others hoped that by helping someone now, they would deserve care when they became old and dependent.

When people care for an elderly relative, they often do not use available community services, such as adult day-care centers. If the caregivers are adult children, they are more likely to use such services, especially because they often have jobs and other responsibilities. In contrast, a spouse, usually the wife, is much less likely to use support services or to put the dependent person in a nursing home. Social workers discovered that the wife normally tries to take care of her husband herself for as long as she can in order not to use up their life savings.

Researchers have found that caring for the elderly can be a very positive experience. The elderly appreciated the care and attention they received. They were affectionate and cooperative. However, even when caregiving is satisfying, it is hard work. Social workers and experts on aging offer caregivers and potential caregivers help when arranging for the care of an elderly relative. One consideration is to ask parents what they want before they become sick or dependent. Perhaps they prefer going into a nursing home, and can select one in advance. On the other hand, they may want to live with their adult children. Caregivers must also

63 learn to be assertive and ask for help from others, espe-
64 cially siblings. Brothers and sisters are often willing to
65 help, but they may not know what to do.
66 We can expect to live longer lives than ever before in
67 American history. Caring for the elderly and being taken
68 care of can be a mutually satisfying experience for ev-
69 eryone involved.

• A. Fact-Finding Exercise

Read the passage again. Read the following statements. Check whether they are True (T) or False (F). If a statement is false, rewrite the statement so that it is true. Then go back to the passage and find the line that supports your answer.

_____ T _____ F 1. Most old people in the United States live in the care of their families.

____

_____ T _____ F 2. Most American couples over 40 have no living parents.

____

_____ T _____ F 3. Elderly people may need care for a long time because they live longer after an illness than they did in the past.

____

_____ T _____ F 4. All caregivers believe someone else can do the job better than they can.

____

_____ T _____ F 5. A spouse is more likely to use community services or put the dependent person in a nursing home.

____

_____ T _____ F 6. Caregiving is easy work when the elderly person is affectionate and cooperative.

____

_____ T _____ F 7. Psychologists and social workers are studying caregiving because Americans live longer today.

____

• B. Reading Analysis

Read each question carefully. Either circle the letter of the correct answer, or write your answer in the space provided.

1. What is the main idea of the passage?
   a. Most old people are put into nursing homes by their families, who do not visit them regularly.
   b. Most old people live longer today after an illness than people did years ago.
   c. Most elderly people are taken care of by their families, who often find the experience satisfying.
2. Read lines 2–3. **Over 80%** means
   a. exactly 80%
   b. between 80% and 100%
   c. more than 80% but less than 90%
3. Read lines 6–14. When is **middle age**?
   a. after 30
   b. after 40
   c. after 50
4. Read lines 16–21. In line 17, "When they do, . . .", what does **they do** mean?
   a. They need care.
   b. They die too.
   c. They have elderly parents.
5. Read lines 24–31.
   a. What follows the colon (:)?
      1. an example
      2. an explanation
      3. a definition
   b. In lines 29–30, what does **regardless of the reason** mean?
      1. The reason was important.
      2. The reason wasn't important.

6. a. Read lines 40–50. What is a **community service**?

   ____

   b. How do you know?

   ____

   c. In line 42, what are **adult children**?

      1. children who have elderly parents
      2. adults with small children
      3. children over 18 years old

   d. In line 45, what is a **spouse**?

   ____

   e. How do you know?

   ____

   f. In lines 44–45, **in contrast** indicates that the information in the following sentence

      1. is the same as the information in the previous sentence
      2. is different from the information in the previous sentence

7. Read lines 54–55. What does **even when** mean?

   a. although
   b. every time
   c. in addition

8. Read lines 59–62. What follows **on the other hand**?

   a. a positive idea
   b. a similar idea
   c. an opposite idea

9. Read lines 64–65. What are **siblings**?

   a. caregivers
   b. brothers and sisters
   c. mothers and fathers

10. Read lines 67–69. In a **mutually satisfying experience**,

    a. the elderly are satisfied, but the caregivers aren't
    b. the caregivers are satisfied, but the elderly aren't
    c. both the elderly and the caregivers are satisfied

• C. Information Organization

Read the passage again. Underline what you think are the main ideas. Then scan the reading and complete the following outline, using the sentences that you have underlined to help you. You will use this outline later to answer questions about the reading.

I.

   A. Family members provide over 80% of the care
   B.

II.

   A. The Average Middle-Aged American Still Has Parents Living
   B.
   C.
   D.

III. Research Findings on Caregiving

   A.
   B. Reasons for This Belief
      1.
      2.
      3.
   C. Three Basic Reasons for Taking on Caregiving Responsibilities
      1.
      2.
      3.

IV. Caregiver Use of Community Services and Nursing Homes

   A. Adult Children:
      Reason:

   B. Spouses:
      Reason:

V. The Experience of Caregiving

   A.
   B.

VI. Factors to Consider in Caregiving

   A.
   B.

• D. Information Recall and Summary

Read each question carefully. Use your outline to answer the questions. Do not refer back to the passage. When you are finished, write a brief summary of the reading.

1. Who cares for the elderly in the United States today?

   ____

2. How is the American family changing today?

   ____

   ____

   ____

3. What is the common characteristic that all caregivers share?

   ____

4. What are the three basic reasons for caregiving?

   a. ______________________________

   b. ______________________________

   c. ______________________________

5. Why are adult children more likely to use community services to help care for an elderly parent?

   ____

6. Why don't most people put their dependent spouses into nursing homes?

   ____

7. a. What advice do social workers give to people when they arrange for the care of an elderly relative?

   ____

   b. What can caregivers do to make their jobs easier?

   ____

Summary

Work in pairs or alone. Write a brief summary of the reading, and put it on the blackboard. Compare your summary with your classmates'. Which one best describes the main idea of the reading?

____

____

____

____

____

• E. Word Forms

Part I

In English, verbs change to adjectives in several ways. Some verbs become adjectives by adding the suffix *-ive*—for example, *demonstrate* (v.) becomes *demonstrative* (adj.).

Complete each sentence with the correct form of the words on the left. **Use the correct tense of the verb in either the affirmative or the negative form.**

cooperate (v.) cooperative (adj.)	1. a. Sometimes small children ________ with the dentist when they have a checkup be cause they are frightened. b. As they become older, however, children become more ____________ because they understand that the dentist will not hurt them.
appreciate (v.) appreciative (adj.)	2. a. Monica is always very ____________ when anyone helps her. b. For example, she _________ her brother's help in painting her living room last month.
assert (v.) assertive (adj.)	3. a. Adrian was very shy and rarely _______ himself. b. He finally learned to become __________ by going to a counselor.
attract (v.) attractive (adj.)	4. a. Effie ___________ a lot of attention in her new dress at the party tomorrow. b. She is quite an ___________ woman, and the dress is an unusual style.
select (v.) selective (adj.)	5. a. Maryanne is very ____________ about the clothes she buys. b. For instance, she only ___________ natural fabrics, such as cotton and wool.

Part 2

In English, verbs change to nouns in several ways. Some verbs become nouns by adding the suffix *-ment*—for example, *disappoint* (v.) becomes *disappointment* (n.).

Complete each sentence with the correct form of the words on the left. **Use the correct tense of the verb in either the affirmative or the negative. Use the singular or plural form of the noun.**

improve (v.) improvement (n.)	1. a. Tom and Nancy's house needs some basic ______________. b. They ____________ the outside now and will work on the inside next year.
place (v.) placement (n.)	2. a. The college __________ new students into different levels of math and English classes. b. The scores on an English and a math test determine the individual ___________ of each student.
arrange (v.) arrangement (n.)	3. a. When Maggie gets married, she will make the necessary ____________ for the church and the restaurant. b. She ______________ for a photographer, though, because her brother will take all the pictures.
require (v.) requirement (n.)	4. a. The Sunset Restaurant ____________ a tie and jacket. People can go there in casual clothes. b. The only ___________ are a shirt and shoes. No bare feet!
state (v.) statement (n.)	5. a. The Governor made some surprising ______________ at his press conference last night. b. He unexpectedly ______________ that he was going to run for President in the next election.

• F. Vocabulary in Context

common (adj.)	eventually (adv.)	obligation (n.)
consideration (n.)	in contrast	perhaps (adv.)
dependent (adj.)	mutual (adj.)	statistic (n.)
elderly (adj.)		

Read the following sentences. Complete each blank space with the correct word or phrase from the list above. Use each word or phrase only once.

1. There are many ______________ people in the United States who live happy, independent lives after they retire.

2. I can't help you. Speak to the Director. ______________ she can help you with your problem.

3. Bob and I have a ________________ agreement. I feed his cat and water his plants when he goes on vacation, and he does the same for me.

4. An American female who is born today can expect to live 78 years, compared to 71 years for a female born in 1950. This ______________ shows the change in how long people can live.

5. People who ride on buses have a _____________ complaint. They do not like waiting outside in bad weather for the bus to come.

6. When Angela began studying computer science, she knew very little, but __________________ she mastered the computer and started to write her own programs.

7. When you accept a job, you have an __________________ to be on time and to do your work well.

8. Margaret became very sick, and she was ________________ on her family for assistance because she could not take care of herself.

9. An American male born today can expect to live 71 years. __________________ an American male born in 1950 can expect to live only 65 years.

10. Debbie and Mark want to buy a house. One ______________ is the size of the house. Another is the quality of the neighborhood.

• G. Topics for Discussion and Writing

1. Who takes care of the elderly in your country? Does the government help? If so, how?
2. In the United States, women are more often caregivers than men. Is this also true in your country? Please explain.
3. Have you ever taken care of a dependent relative? Describe the experience. What did you learn from it?

• H. Follow-Up Activities

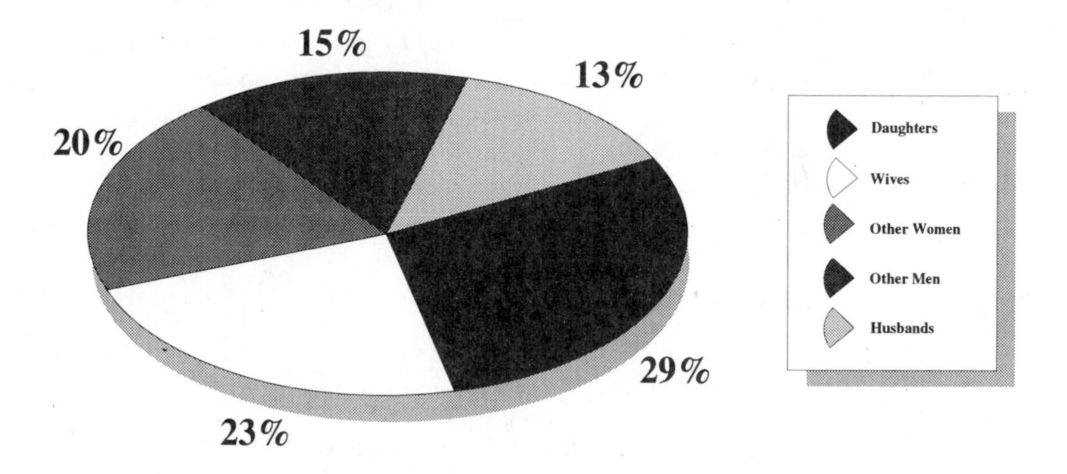

1. Refer to the pie chart above, and answer the following questions.
   a. In the United States, who is most likely to be a caregiver?

   ____

   b. Who is least likely to be a caregiver?

   ____

   c. What are some reasons that can explain this?

   ____

   d. What percent of caregivers are women?

   ____

   e. What percent of caregivers are men?

   ____

   f. What are some reasons that can explain this difference?

   ____

   ____

LIVING ARRANGEMENTS FOR AMERICANS 65 YEARS AND OLDER

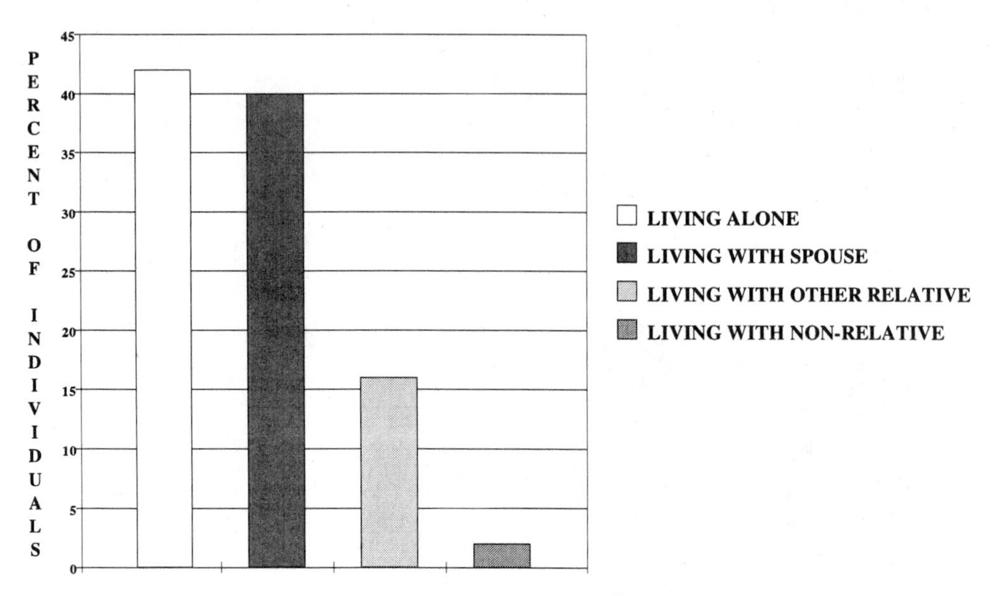

2. Refer to the bar graph above, and answer the following questions.
   a. What percent of older Americans are living with other relatives?

      ____

   b. What percent of older Americans are living alone?

      ____

   c. What percent of older Americans are living with non-relatives?

      ____

   d. Who do you think these non-relatives are?

      ____

3. Imagine that you are old and unable to take care of yourself. Answer the following questions. When you are finished, discuss your answers with your classmates. Are your answers similar? Different?
   a. Whom do you want to take care of you? A relative? A nurse? Someone else? Why?
   b. Where do you want to live? In your own home? In a relative's home? In a nursing home? Why?

4. Refer to the questionnaire on the following page. Go out alone or in pairs. Survey two or three people. Then bring back your data and combine it with your classmates' information. How do these results compare with the answers you discussed in class? Can you make any general statements about the results of your survey? Do people from the same country have similar ideas about care of the elderly?

Survey: Care of the Elderly

	Respondent #1	Respondent #2	Respondent #3
gender			
nationality			
age			
Who would you prefer as your caregiver in your old age?			
Where do you want to live when you are over 65?			
What are your reasons for these decisions?			

Unit II Review

• I. Crossword Puzzle

Clues

Across

2. start
5. not simple; sophisticated
6. Coca-Cola is a ______ drink. Many people like it.
8. Very young children _____ before they can make real words.
10. the past of *get*
13. ______ are people who study language.
14. A _____ is a person who takes care of another person.
16. brothers and sisters
18. the opposite of *down*
19. different
21. the opposite of *yes*
23. When people work together, they need to ______.
24. a husband or wife
25. ability
29. after a time

Down

1. the opposite of *start*
3. In people, the abilities to speak and to walk are ______.
4. sickness; disease
5. I ______ do this crossword puzzle.
7. I like you, and you like me. Our feelings are ______.
8. man, woman, ______, girl
9. ______ is a sad feeling of being alone.
11. Mary watched her cat carefully in order to make an ______ about her cat's behavior.
12. different
15. opposite of *out*
17. People who participate in an experiment are called ______.
20. by yourself; no one else is with you
22. assist
23. usual
24. choose; pick
26. allow; permit
27. the past of *have*
28. sick; not well
30. the opposite of *bottom*

• J. Unit II Discussion

The three topics in this unit discuss the way different people cope with living in society. How do you think language skills, loneliness, and care of the elderly are related? How do they affect each other?

Unit III

Justice and Crime

C·H·A·P·T·E·R 7

Innocent Until Proven Guilty: The Criminal Court System

• Prereading Preparation

1. In groups of three or four, discuss the job of the police. What do you think their responsibilities should be? What should they have the authority to do?

2. Read the title of this chapter. In the American legal system, a person accused of a crime is considered to be innocent until he or she is proven guilty in court. In your country, does an accused person have to prove his or her innocence, or does the court have to prove the person's guilt?

3. Refer to the photo on page 93.The woman represents justice. Why is she blindfolded? What do the scales in her left hand symbolize? What does the sword in her right hand symbolize?

1 The purpose of the American court system is to pro-
2 tect the rights of the people. According to American law,
3 if someone is accused of a crime, he is considered inno-
4 cent until the court proves that the person is guilty. In
5 other words, it is the responsibility of the court to prove
6 that a person is guilty. It is not the responsibility of the
7 person to prove that he or she is innocent.
8 In order to arrest a person, the police have to be rea-
9 sonably sure that a crime has been committed. The po-
10 lice must give the suspect the reasons why they are
11 arresting him and tell him his rights under the law.[1]
12 Then the police take the suspect to the police station to
13 "book" him. "Booking" means that the name of the per-

[1]The police must say, "You have the right to remain silent. Anything you say can and will be used against you in a court of law. You have the right to speak to a lawyer and to have the lawyer present during questioning. If you so desire, and cannot afford one, a lawyer will be appointed without any charge before any questioning. Do you understand these rights as I have explained them to you?" These rights are called the Miranda rights.

14 son and the charges against him are formally listed at
15 the police station.
16 The next step is for the suspect to go before a judge.
17 The judge decides whether the suspect should be kept
18 in jail or released. If the suspect has no previous crimi-
19 nal record and the judge feels that he will return to
20 court rather than run away—for example, because he
21 owns a house and has a family—he can go free. Other-
22 wise, the suspect must put up bail.[2] At this time, too,
23 the judge will appoint a court lawyer to defend the sus-
24 pect if he can't afford one.
25 The suspect returns to court a week or two later. A
26 lawyer from the district attorney's office presents a case
27 against the suspect. This is called a hearing. The attor-
28 ney may present evidence as well as witnesses. The
29 judge at the hearing then decides whether there is
30 enough reason to hold a trial. If the judge decides that
31 there is sufficient evidence to call for a trial, he or she
32 sets a date for the suspect to appear in court to formally
33 plead guilty or not guilty.
34 At the trial, a jury of 12 people listens to the evi-
35 dence from both attorneys and hears the testimony of
36 the witnesses. Then the jury goes into a private room to
37 consider the evidence and decide whether the defen-
38 dant is guilty of the crime. If the jury decides that the
39 defendant is innocent, he goes free. However, if he is
40 convicted, the judge sets a date for the defendant to ap-
41 pear in court again for sentencing. At this time, the
42 judge tells the convicted person what his punishment
43 will be. The judge may sentence him to prison, order
44 him to pay a fine, or place him on probation.[3]
45 The American justice system is very complex and
46 sometimes operates slowly. However, every step is de-
47 signed to protect the rights of the people. These indi-
48 vidual rights are the basis, or foundation, of the
49 American government.

[2] Bail is an amount of money which the accused person pays to the court to assure that he will return to the court on the trial date. If the person comes back, the money is returned to him. If not, the court keeps the bail money.

[3] Probation means that the convicted person does not have to go to jail. Instead, he must follow certain rules, and is supervised by a parole officer.

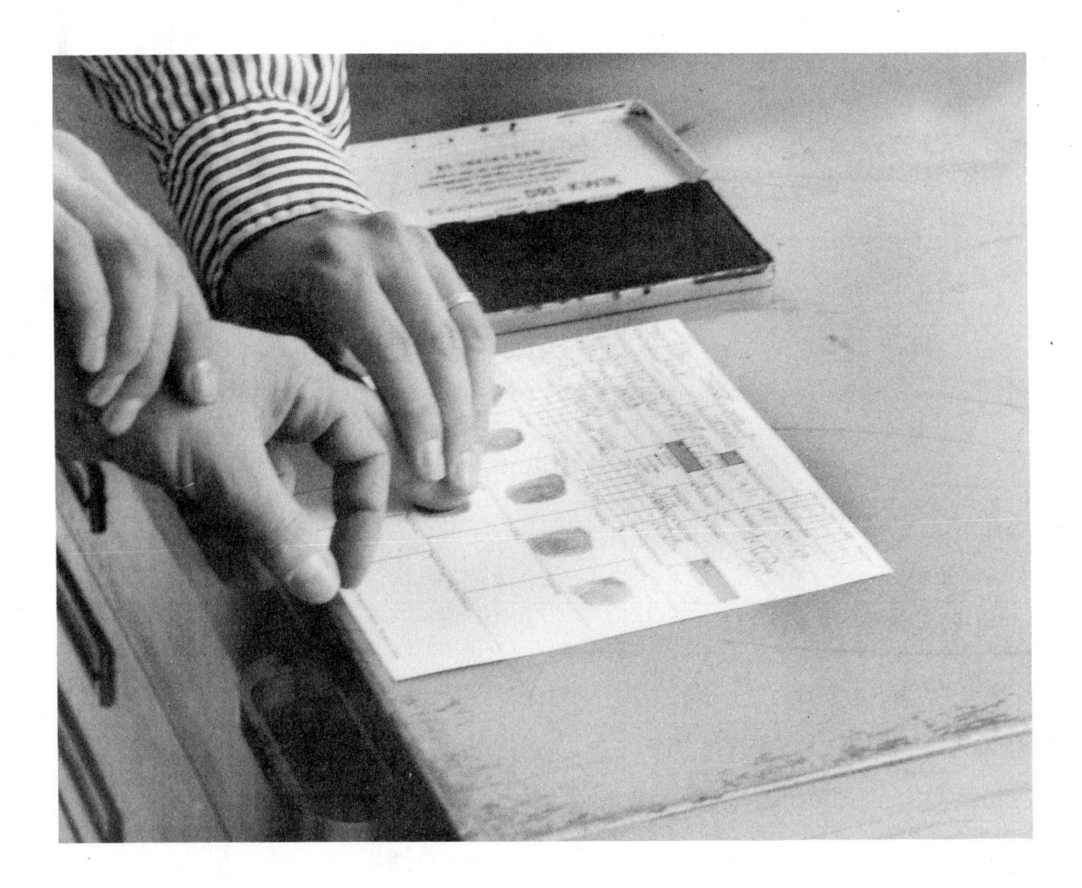

• A. Fact-Finding Exercise

Read the passage again. Read the following statements. Check whether they are True (T) or False (F). If a statement is false, rewrite the statement so that it is true. Then go back to the passage and find the line that supports your answer.

_____ T _____ F 1. According to American law, the court must prove that a suspect is innocent.

____

_____ T _____ F 2. The police decide if a suspect stays in jail or can be released.

____

_____ T _____ F 3. The judge appoints a court lawyer for a suspect who cannot pay for one.

____

_____ T _____ F 4. An attorney can present evidence or witnesses at the hearing.

____

_____ T _____ F 5. There are 12 people on a jury.

____

_____ T _____ F 6. At a trial, the judge decides if the suspect is guilty or innocent.

____

_____ T _____ F 7. The jury gives the convicted person his punishment after the trial.

____

• B. Reading Analysis

Read each question carefully. Either circle the letter of the correct answer, or write your answer in the space provided.

1. What is the main idea of the passage?

    a. According to the American court system, a suspect must prove that she or he is innocent.
    b. The American court system is very complex and was designed to protect the rights of the people.
    c. According to the American court system, a judge decides if a suspect is innocent or guilty.

2. Read lines 3–4: ". . . he is considered innocent. . . ." This means

    a. the law thinks the suspect is innocent
    b. the law must prove the suspect is innocent

3. Read lines 4–6. What follows **in other words**?

    a. an example of the previous sentence
    b. a restatement of the previous sentence
    c. a new idea about the court system

4. Read lines 8–9. **Reasonably sure** means

    a. very sure
    b. not sure
    c. a little sure

5. a. Read the sentence in lines 9–11: "The police. . . tell him his rights under the law." What are these rights called?

   ____

   b. How do you know?

   ____

   c. This information is called a

      1. direction
      2. footnote
      3. preface

6. Read lines 12–15.

   a. In line 13, what does **"booking"** mean?

   ____

   b. Why does this word have quotation marks (**" "**) around it?

      1. It is a new word.
      2. Someone is saying this word in the reading.
      3. It is a special meaning of the word *book* that the police use.

7. Read lines 16–24.

   a. **He can go free** means

      1. the suspect is not guilty
      2. the suspect does not have to go to trial because the judge has decided he is innocent
      3. the suspect does not have to wait in jail or pay money until he goes to trial

   b. **Otherwise** means

      1. if not
      2. in addition
      3. in contrast

   c. Read the footnote describing **bail.** What is the purpose of having the suspect pay bail?

      1. to pay for the judge and the trial
      2. as insurance that the suspect will return to court
      3. to pay for a court lawyer to defend the suspect

8. Read lines 25–27. What is a **hearing**?

   ____

9. Read lines 28–33. What is a synonym for **enough reason**?

____

10. In line 39, **however** means

    a. also
    b. next
    c. but

11. Read lines 39–44.

    a. What is **sentencing**?
        1. subjects, verbs, and objects
        2. the date the defendant must appear in court
        3. the punishment that the judge gives the defendant

    b. Read the footnote about **probation.** What is the purpose of probation?

        1. to make sure the convicted person behaves well
        2. to save the court some money

12. a. Read lines 47–49. What is a synonym for **basis**?

    ____

    b. How do you know?

    ____

    ____

• C. Information Organization

Read the passage again. Underline what you think are the main ideas. Then scan the reading and complete the following flowchart, using the sentences that you have underlined to help you. You will use this flowchart later to answer questions about the reading.

THE AMERICAN JUSTICE SYSTEM

POLICE ARREST SUSPECT AND READ MIRANDA RIGHTS

SUSPECT GOES BEFORE A JUDGE

SUSPECT PUTS UP BAIL

SUSPECT WAITS IN JAIL FOR HEARING
JUDGE APPOINTS A COURT LAWYER

SUSPECT APPEARS IN COURT FOR HEARING
DISTRICT ATTORNEY PRESENTS CASE AGAINST SUSPECT

IS SENTENCED

• D. Information Recall and Summary

Read each question carefully. Use your flowchart to answer the questions. Do not refer back to the passage. When you are finished, write a brief summary of the reading.

1. What must the police do after they arrest a suspect?

____

____

____

____

____

2. What happens to the suspect after the police book him?

____

____

____

____

3. What happens at a trial? Describe it.

____

____

4. If a person is proven innocent, what happens?

____

5. If a person is convicted, what happens?

____

Summary

Work in pairs or alone. Write a brief summary of the reading, and put it on the blackboard. Compare your summary with your classmates'. Which one best describes the main idea of the reading?

____

____

____

____

____

• E. Word Forms

Part 1

In English, adjectives become nouns in several ways. Some verbs become nouns by adding the suffix *-ment*—for example, *govern* becomes (v.), *government* (n.).

Complete each sentence with the correct form of the words on the left. **Use the correct tense of the verb in either the affirmative or the negative form. Use the singular or plural form of the noun.**

appoint (v.) appointment (n.)	1. a. In a few weeks, the President __________ a new ambassador to Japan. b. This is a very important __________ because Japan is an economically powerful country.
punish (v.) punishment (n.)	2. a. In the American court system, a judge tries to make the __________ fit the crime. b. For instance, a judge __________ a convicted person with life in prison for stealing a bicycle.
establish (v.) establishment (n.)	3. a. In the United States, the permanent __________ of a democratic government took several years. b. The United States __________ a constitutional government in 1787.
disagree (v.) disagreement (n.)	4. a. Allison and Clark had several __________ about redecorating their home. b. In fact, they __________ on almost everything: paint color, furniture, carpets, and lights.
judge (v.) judgment (n.)	5. a. A person who __________ a trial must be impartial when making decisions. b. In a court of law, __________ must be made fairly and objectively.

Part 2

In English, some adjectives become nouns by adding the suffix *-ity*—for example, *national* (adj.), becomes *nationality* (n.).

Complete each sentence with the correct form of the words on the left. **Use the singular or the plural form of the noun.**

responsible (adj.)
responsibility (n.)

1. a. Employees have many __________ to their employers.
   b. Employees are usually __________ for coming to work on time, for being productive at work, and for being honest with their employer.

formal (adj.)
formality (n.)

2. a. On very __________ occasions, especially when they go out, Americans like to dress up.
   b. However, at home, Americans do not observe the same __________. For example, men usually do not wear a suit to go to a friend's house for dinner.

complex (adj.)
complexity (n.)

3. a. Today, a car is quite a __________ machine. New cars have computers and electronic fuel systems.
   b. In the past, however, cars were much simpler. __________ in machinery developed over many years as technology advanced.

individual (adj.)
individuality (n.)

4. a. In general, people value their __________.
   b. Even when they are part of a group, people enjoy making __________ decisions.

public (adj.)
publicity (n.)

5. a. The mayor made a very unpopular __________ announcement yesterday.
   b. He received considerable negative __________ when he announced that he planned to reduce many city services.

• F. Dictionary Skills

Read the following sentences. Use the context to help you understand the boldface words. Read the dictionary entry for that word and choose the appropriate definition. Then rewrite the sentence, using the definition you have chosen. Be sure to make your sentence grammatically correct.

1. The police list the **charges** against a suspect in a book at the police station.

charge *n* **1** accusation; statement that a person has done wrong, esp. that he has broken a law. **2** sudden and violent attack at high speed (by soldiers, animals, a football player, etc.). **3** price asked for goods or services: *hotel ~s.* **4** care, responsibility.

___

2. The police may not have any **record** of criminal activity for a particular suspect.

record *n* **1** written account of facts, events, etc.: *a ~ of school attendances.* **2** state of being recorded or preserved in writing, esp. as authentic evidence: *a matter of ~*, something that is established as fact. **3** facts known about the past of a person or something: *He has an honorable ~ of service.* **4** something that provides evidence or information: *Our museums are full of ~s of past history.*

___

3. The judge's first **step** is to decide whether to keep the suspect in jail or to allow him to go free until the hearing.

step *n* **1** act of stepping once; distance covered by doing this. **2** sound made by somebody walking. **3** one action in a series of actions in order to do something. **4** grade, rank.

___

4. The district attorney's office **presents** evidence against a suspect.

present *v* **1** give; offer. **2** appear; come forward. **3** show; display. **4** bring (a play, film, radio or television program, etc.) before the public.

___

5. The jury goes into a private room in order to **consider** the evidence against the suspect, and decide whether the suspect is innocent or guilty.

consider *v* **1** think about. **2** take into account. **3** be of the opinion; regard as.

___

• G. Vocabulary in Context

Read the following sentences. Complete each blank space with the correct word or phrase from the list above. Use each word only once.

appoint (v.)	establish (v.)	present (v.)
basis (n.)	however (adv.)	purpose (n.)
case (n.)	otherwise (adv.)	record (n.)
consider (v.)		

1. The Board of Health keeps an accurate __________ of all births and deaths in the city.
2. Holly worked very hard before she was able to __________ her own business, but eventually she was successful.
3. If it snows this week, we will go skiing this weekend. __________ we will stay in the city and see a movie.
4. The students always __________ a class representative for the student council at the beginning of the semester.
5. Every fall, television stations __________ new programs to their viewers.
6. When deciding on a college, you need to __________ several factors, including the cost of tuition, the courses offered, and the location of the college.
7. The ability to read and write well is the __________ of a good education.
8. I don't understand the __________ of this machine. What is it used for?
9. I prefer to eat only fresh vegetables. __________, when they are not available, I eat frozen or canned vegetables.
10. Have you read about the killing in the library last year? The police have been trying to solve that murder __________ for months, but so far they haven't been successful.

• H. Topics for Discussion and Writing

1. Work in small groups. The government has asked you to review the present procedure for arresting and booking a suspect. Review the steps involved in arresting and charging a person with a crime. Discuss what you would and would not change. Present your revised procedure to the class.
2. In the United States, trials are not held in secret. The public may sit in the courtroom and observe the proceedings. Visit a courtroom with two or three of your classmates. Observe what takes place. Report back to the class.

• I. Follow-Up Activities

1. Refer to the chart in Exercise C, which lists for the American procedure for arresting and trying a person for a crime. Compare this system with the system in your country. Using the following chart, compare the two systems and write what you see as the advantages and disadvantages of each.

	In the United States	In ________
Procedure		
Advantage		
Disadvantage		
Procedure		
Advantage		
Disadvantage		
Procedure		
Advantage		
Disadvantage		

2. Read about a criminal case in the news. Bring several newspaper and magazine articles on the case into class. In groups, form juries. Read through the evidence and decide whether the suspect is guilty or innocent. If your group decides the suspect is guilty, appoint a judge from your group to decide on a sentence.

C·H·A·P·T·E·R 8

The Reliability of Eyewitnesses

• Prereading Preparation

1. Look at the photograph on the left. Where was this photograph taken? Who are the four women? Why are they there? Who are the two people sitting down? Who is the woman pointing to? Why?
2. What kinds of evidence are used to convict criminals? In small groups, use the chart below to make a list of the kinds of evidence used to convict criminals for the crimes listed.

Crime	Murder	Bank Robbery	Mugging
Types of Evidence			

3. In your country, what kinds of evidence are used to convict criminals for these crimes?
4. In your country, is an eyewitness's testimony important in convicting criminals?
5. In your opinion, what kinds of people make reliable eyewitnesses? Why?

Bernard Jackson is a free man today, but he has many bitter memories. Jackson spent five years in prison after a jury wrongly convicted him of raping two women. At Jackson's trial, although two witnesses testified that Jackson was with them in another location at the times of the crimes, he was convicted anyway. Why? The jury believed the testimony of the two victims, who positively identified Jackson as the man who had attacked them. The court eventually freed Jackson after the police found the man who had really committed the crimes. Jackson was similar in appearance to the guilty man. The two women had made a mistake in identity. As a result, Jackson has lost five years of his life.

The two women in this case were eyewitnesses. They clearly saw the man who attacked them, yet they mistakenly identified an innocent person. Similar incidents have occurred before. Eyewitnesses to other crimes have identified the wrong person in a police lineup or in photographs.

Many factors influence the accuracy of eyewitness testimony. For instance, witnesses sometimes see photographs of several suspects before they try to identify the person they saw in a lineup of people. They can become confused by seeing many photographs of similar faces. The number of people in the lineup, and whether it is a live lineup or a photograph, may also affect a witness's decision. People sometimes have difficulty identifying people of other races. The questions the police ask witnesses also have an effect on them.

Are some witnesses more reliable than others? Many people believe that police officers are more reliable than ordinary people. Psychologists decided to test this idea, and they discovered that it is not true. Two psychologists showed a film of crimes to both police officers and civilians. The psychologists found no difference between the police and the civilians in correctly remembering the details of the crimes.

Despite all the possibilities for inaccuracy, courts cannot exclude eyewitness testimony from a trial. American courts depend almost completely on eyewitness testimony to resolve court cases. Sometimes it is the only evidence to a crime, such as rape. Furthermore, eyewitness testimony is often correct. Although people do sometimes make mistakes, many times they really do identify individuals correctly.

American courts depend on the ability of the twelve jurors, and not the judges, to determine the accuracy of the witness's testimony. It is their responsibility to decide if a certain witness could actually see, hear, and remember what occurred.

In a few cases the testimony of eyewitnesses has convicted innocent people. More importantly, it has rightly convicted a larger number of guilty people; consequently, it continues to be of great value in the American judicial system.

• A. Fact-Finding Exercise

Read the passage again. Read the following statements. Check whether they are True (T) or False (F). If a statement is false, rewrite the statement so that it is true. Then go back to the passage and find the line that supports your answer.

_____ T _____ F 1. Bernard Jackson went to jail for five years because he was guilty.

____

_____ T _____ F 2. Bernard Jackson looked like the guilty man, but he was innocent.

____

_____ T _____ F 3. The eyewitnesses in Jackson's trial were wrong.

____

_____ T _____ F 4. Some witnesses become confused when they see too many photographs of similar people.

____

_____ T _____ F 5. Police officers are better witnesses than ordinary people.

____

_____ T _____ F 6. American courts depend a lot on eyewitness testimony.

____

_____ T _____ F 7. The judge must decide if a witness's story is accurate.

____

• B. Reading Analysis

Read each question carefully. Either circle the letter of the correct answer, or write your answer in the space provided.

1. What is the main idea of the passage?

   a. Bernard Jackson spent five years in jail, but he was innocent.
   b. Eyewitness testimony, although sometimes incorrect, is valuable.
   c. Police officers are not better eyewitnesses than civilians.

2. According to the passage, which of the following factors influence eyewitnesses? Check the correct ones.

   ___ a. seeing many similar photographs
   ___ b. the time of day the crime happened
   ___ c. the questions the police ask
   ___ d. the age and sex of the witness
   ___ e. a live lineup or a photograph of a group of people
   ___ f. the type of job the witness has
   ___ g. the education of the witness
   ___ h. the race of the suspect

3. Read lines 1–2. What are **bitter memories**?

   a. angry memories
   b. unhappy memories
   c. prison memories

4. Read lines 7–8.

   a. What does **testimony** mean?

      1. a written statement used for evidence
      2. a photograph used for evidence
      3. an oral statement used for evidence

   b. What does **victims** refer to?

      1. the people who commit a crime
      2. the people against whom a crime is committed

5. a. In line 15, what does **yet** mean?

      1. after
      2. so
      3. but

   b. How do you know?

   ____

6. In line 21, what does **for instance** mean?

   a. in addition
   b. for example
   c. however

7. Read lines 30–37: ". . . they discovered that it is not true."

   a. What is not true? It is not true that

   ____

   b. What are **civilians**?

      1. police officers
      2. ordinary people
      3. psychologists

8. Read lines 38–43.

   a. What does **despite** mean?

      1. in addition to
      2. as a result
      3. in spite of

   b. What does **evidence** mean?

      1. proof
      2. result
      3. story

9. Read lines 48–50: "It is their responsibility to decide if . . . ."

   Who does **their** refer to?

   a. the judges
   b. the courts
   c. the jurors

10. Read lines 53–54. What does **consequently** mean?

   a. as a result
   b. however
   c. in addition

DETECTIVE BUREAU PHOTOGRAPHIC UNIT	POLICE DEPARTMENT CITY OF METROPOLIS	PLEASE POST IN A CONSPICUOUS PLACE

WANTED

FOR ARMED ROBBERY

THE ABOVE IS A SKETCH RESEMBLING A SUSPECT SOUGHT FOR AN ARMED ROBBERY THAT OCCURRED ON DECEMBER 6, 1994 AT 0125 HRS IN THE CONFINES OF THE 13TH PRECINCT. THIS SKETCH IS BASED ON A DESCRIPTION SUPPLIED BY THE VICTIM.

DESCRIPTION: MALE WHITE, 40-45 YEARS, APPROXIMATE HEIGHT 6' 2", 160 LBS, MEDIUM LENGTH BROWN HAIR, WEARING A BEIGE , SLEEVELESS POCKET VEST.

THE ABOVE SUBJECT, WITH AT LEAST FIVE OTHERS, OVERTOOK A SECURITY GUARD AT GUNPOINT, TYING HIM UP WITH ROPE IN A PARKING LOT AT 4TH AND MAIN STREETS. THEY THEN REMOVED SIX TRUCKS LOADED WITH OVER ONE MILLION DOLLARS WORTH OF DESIGNER CLOTHING. SUSPECT AND HIS ASSOCIATES ARE TO BE CONSIDERED ARMED AND DANGEROUS, AND WELL DRESSED.

CASE NUMBER: 1994-4035-22

CIRCULAR NO. 94/115 DATE PREPARED 02/13/94	POLICE DEPARTMENT CITY OF METROPOLIS	LIMITED TO DEPARTMENT CIRCULATION

Refer to the wanted poster above. In small groups, answer the following questions.

1. Who is this man?
2. Who drew this picture?
3. What do the police think this man did?
4. Where can you see wanted posters?

• C. Information Organization

Read the passage again. Underline what you think are the main ideas. Then scan the reading and complete the following outline, using the sentences that you have underlined to help you. You will use this outline later to answer questions about the reading.

I. Bernard Jackson's Case

A. His Crime:

B. The Evidence:

C. Reason for His Conviction:

D. The Problem:

II. Factors Influencing the Accuracy of Eyewitness Testimony

A.

B.

C.

D.

E. The Questions the Police Ask Witnesses Have an Effect on Them

III. Experiment to Test the Reliability of Police Officers and Ordinary People as Witnesses

A. Experiment:

B. Results:

IV. Why Courts Cannot Exclude Eyewitness Testimony from a Trial

A.

B.

• D. Information Recall and Summary

Read each question carefully. Use your outline to answer the questions. Do not refer back to the passage. When you are finished, write a brief summary of the reading.

1. Why did Bernard Jackson go to prison? Was he guilty?

   ____

2. At Jackson's trial, what did the two witnesses testify? Did the jury believe the two witnesses?

   ____

   ____

3. Why did the victims identify Jackson as the man who had attacked them?

   ____

4. What are some factors that affect eyewitness testimony?

   ____

   ____

5. a. Are police officers better witnesses than ordinary people?

   ____

   b. How did psychologists test this idea?

   ____

6. Why is eyewitness testimony important in an American court?

   ____

7. In an American court, who decides if the eyewitness testimony is correct or not? Why is eyewitness testimony a valuable part of the American judicial system?

   ____

   ____

Summary

Work in pairs or alone. Write a brief summary of the reading, and put it on the blackboard. Compare your summary with your classmates'. Which one best describes the main idea of the reading?

____

____

____

____

• E. Word Forms

Part 1

In English, there are several ways verbs change to nouns. Some verbs become nouns by adding the suffix *-ence* or *-ance*—for example, *insist* (v.) becomes *insistence* (n.).

Complete each sentence with the correct form of the words on the left. **Use the correct tense of the verb in either the affirmative or the negative form. Use the singular or plural form of the noun.**

depend (v.) dependence (n.)	1. a. When a baby is born, it __________ on its parents completely. b. As it grows up, the child's __________ on its parents decreases.
differ (v.) difference (n.)	2. a. Angela's coat and Debbie's coat __________ in color. They are both blue. b. The only __________ between the two coats are their size and material.
occur (v.) occurrence (n.)	3. a. Snow in April is an unusual __________ in this area. b. In fact, snow __________ very often, even in the winter. Only two or three inches falls during the entire season.
appear (v.) appearance (n.)	4. a. The President made a special __________ on television last night. b. He __________ very calm, but his news was serious.
assist (v.) assistance (n.)	5. a. The nurses __________ the doctor today, but they will help her during the operation tomorrow. b. The doctor will need their __________ to give her surgical instruments.

Part 2

In English, the verb and noun forms of some words are the same—for example, *change* (n.) and *change* (v.).

Complete each sentence with the correct form of the word on the left. **Use the correct tense of the verb in either the affirmative or the negative form. Use the singular or plural form of the noun. In addition, indicate whether you are using the noun (n.) or verb (v.) form.**

influence

1. a. Many people believe that the weather ________ *(n., v.)* our feelings.
   b. However the strength of this ________ *(n., v.)* has not been proven.

film

2. a. Unfortunately, John ________ *(n., v.)* our high school reunion next month.
   b. His ________ *(n., v.)* of social gatherings are always interesting, so we are very disappointed.

attack

3. a. People frequently write ________ *(n., v.)* on politicians in the newspapers, but the politicians do not always pay attention to them.
   b. People usually ________ *(n., v.)* the politicians' dishonesty.

witness

4. a. Margaret was the only ________ *(n., v.)* to a serious car accident.
   b. As soon as she ________ *(n., v.)* the accident, she called an ambulance and the police.

mistake

5. a. Susan and Emily are twin sisters. People frequently ________ Emily for Susan and Susan for Emily because they look alike.
   (n., v.)

   b. Sometimes such ________ in identity are funny.
   (n., v.)

question

6. a. The police ________ the suspect until his lawyer arrived. The suspect wanted his lawyer to be present.
   (n., v.)

   b. They asked him very specific ________, but his answers were unclear.
   (n., v.)

• F. Dictionary Skills

Read the following sentences. Use the context to help you understand the boldface words. Read the dictionary entry for that word and choose the appropriate definition. Then rewrite the sentence, using the definition you have chosen. Be sure to make your sentence grammatically correct.

1. The number of people in the **lineup**, and whether it is a live lineup or a photograph, may affect a witness's decision.

lineup *n* **1** row of persons placed side-by-side for identification. **2** (list of) players taking part in a game. **3** way in which persons, states, etc. are allied.

---

2. Courts cannot **exclude** eyewitness testimony from a trial. Sometimes it is the only evidence to a crime.

exclude *v* **1** shut or keep out; bar; *~ him from taking part.* **2** ignore; disregard.

---

3. Eyewitness testimony continues to be of **value** in the American judicial system.

value *n* **1** quality of being useful or desirable; *the ~ of walking as an exercise.* **2** worth of something when compared with something else. **3** worth of something in terms of money or other goods for which it can be exchanged. **4** (in music) full time indicated by a note.

---

4. The two women were **positive** that Bernard Jackson had committed the crimes against them.

positive *adj* **1** definite; clearly stated. **2** sure; certain. **3** constructive; helpful; *a ~ suggestion.* **4** favorable; affirmative; *a ~ response.*

• G. Vocabulary in Context

bitter (adj.)	guilty (adj.)	similar (adj.)
civilian (n.)	innocent (adj.)	testimony (n.)
despite (prep.)	mistake (n.)	victims (n.)
evidence (n.)		

Read the following sentences. Complete each blank space with the correct word from the list above. Use each word only once.

1. John was in the army for two years. At the end of his military service, he was happy to become a ______________ again.

2. Last week, an armed robber shot two men when he robbed the City Bank. Afterwards, an ambulance took the two __________ to the hospital.

3. Tommy stole a car, but the police caught and arrested him. Because Tommy was ________________, he went to prison for six months.

4. Kathy saw the two men who robbed City Bank. As a result of her ________________ in court, the two men were convicted and put into prison.

5. When the police investigate a crime, they look for _____________ , such as fingerprints, footprints, hair, and clothing.

6. Mr. Michaels worked for the same company for 25 years. Six months before retiring, he lost his job, and he couldn't find another one. He has become very _____________ towards his old company.

7. Many people believed that Ronald had murdered his wife, but he was _________________.

8. ________________ the cold weather, Kay went to work without her coat.

9. Chris and his brother look very ______________. They are both tall and thin, and both have light hair and blue eyes.

10. The waitress made a ______________. She gave me coffee, but I had ordered tea.

• H. Topics for Discussion and Writing

1. In this article, the two women made a mistake in identity. Think about a case you know of in which an innocent person was convicted of a crime because eyewitnesses made a mistake. Describe the case.
2. Is it possible to be sure of an eyewitness's testimony? Please explain.
3. Have you ever witnessed a crime or an accident? Were you able to remember the exact details? Why or why not? Describe what happened.

• I. Follow-Up Activities

1. Reread lines 20–29 of the article. What can the police do differently to help avoid cases of mistaken identity? With a partner, read the following sets of questions. Decide which one in each pair is the better question for the police to ask. Compare your choices with your classmates' choices. Be prepared to explain your decisions.

   a. ___ 1. What was the suspect wearing?
   ___ 2. Was the suspect wearing a shirt and pants, or a suit?

   b. ___ 1. Did the suspect have a gun or a knife?
   ___ 2. Did the suspect have a weapon? If so, what did you see?

   c. ___ 1. Exactly what did the suspect look like? Describe the suspect's face in detail.
   ___ 2. Will you look at these photographs and tell us which one is a photo of the suspect?

   d. ___ 1. What do you estimate was the suspect's height and weight?
   ___ 2. How tall and heavy was the suspect?

2. In this article, the two women made a mistake in identity. There are many factors that can cause people to make an error. Refer to the chart below. Work in small groups with your classmates. Which factors might confuse people and cause them to make mistakes in identity? Why? Write your reasons and rank the factors in the table below. For example, if you think that **weather** is the factor that would confuse people the most, write **1** next to **weather** under **RANK**.

FACTOR	REASON	RANK
sex (of witness/ of suspect)		
race (of witness/ of suspect)		
age (of witness/ of suspect)		
time of day		
weather		
distance of witness from the crime		
level of education of the witness		

C·H·A·P·T·E·R 9

The Death Penalty in the United States: Old Enough to Kill, Old Enough to Die?

• Prereading Preparation

1. What is the death penalty?
2. What does **old enough to kill, old enough to die** mean?
3. What do you think the author's opinion is? What makes you think this is her opinion?
4. Is there a death penalty in your country? If there is, for what crimes is there a death penalty?
5. In your country, who decides on the penalty for a crime?
6. In your country, who decides on the death penalty?

1 In the United States, 36 states currently allow capital
2 punishment for serious crimes such as murder. Ameri-
3 cans have always argued about the death penalty. To-
4 day, there is a serious question about this issue: Should
5 there be a minimum age limit for executing criminals?
6 In other words, is it right for convicted murders who kill
7 when they are minors—i.e., under the age of 18—to re-
8 ceive the death penalty?
9 In most other countries of the world, there is no
10 capital punishment for minors. In the United States,
11 though, each state makes its own decision. Of the 36
12 states that allow the death penalty, 30 permit the execu-
13 tion of minors.
14 In the state of South Carolina, a convicted murderer
15 was given the death penalty for a crime he committed
16 while he was a minor. In 1977, when he was 17 years
17 old, James Terry Roach and two friends brutally mur-
18 dered three people. Roach's lawyer fought the decision
19 to execute him. The young murderer remained on Death

20 Row (a separate part of prison for convicted criminals
21 who are sentenced to die) for ten years while his lawyer
22 appealed to the governor. The lawyer argued that it is
23 wrong to execute a person for a crime he committed
24 while he was a minor. In the United States, the governor
25 of a state has the power to change a sentence from the
26 death penalty to life in prison. Nonetheless, the gover-
27 nor of South Carolina refused to stop the execution.
28 Roach was finally executed by electrocution in 1986.
29 This is not the first time a criminal was executed in
30 South Carolina for a crime he committed when he was a
31 minor. In 1944, a 14-year-old boy died in that state's
32 electric chair.

33 In Indiana, a 16-year-old girl was on Death Row for a
34 crime she committed when she was 15. Paula Cooper
35 and three friends stabbed an elderly woman to death in
36 1986. They robbed the old woman to get money to play
37 video games. At the time of the murder, the minimum
38 age limit for executions in that state was 10. Cooper's
39 lawyer appealed to the governor of Indiana to stop the
40 execution because the convicted killer was very young
41 and because she was abused in childhood. The Indiana
42 governor, who favors the death penalty, said that he had
43 to let the courts do their job.

44 Two years after Paula Cooper's crime, Indiana raised
45 the minimum age limit for executions to the age of 16.
46 However, the courts still refused to stop Cooper's execu-
47 tion because she had been sentenced before the age
48 limit for executions was changed. In 1988 the U.S. Su-
49 preme Court decided to bar, or prohibit, the execution
50 of juveniles who were under the age of 16 when they
51 committed their crime. Cooper's lawyer again asked the
52 court to stop her execution. Finally, in July of 1989,
53 Paula Cooper was sentenced to 60 years in prison. She is
54 no longer on Death Row.

55 Although no one believes that these killers deserve
56 sympathy, some people believe that capital punishment
57 is too severe for convicted murderers who are minors.
58 They feel that it is wrong to treat minors the same as
60 adults in these cases. Opponents of the death penalty in
61 general think it is wrong to take one life for another.
62 They argue that capital punishment does not protect the
63 victim or the victim's family. Opponents also suggest
64 that, occasionally, innocent people may be executed for
65 crimes they did not commit.

66 On the other hand, people who agree with the death
67 penalty argue that it prevents repeat crimes and, there-
68 fore, future victims. These proponents of capital pun-
69 ishment believe that fear of the death penalty deters
70 crime. That is, fewer people will commit murder be-
71 cause they fear the death penalty.
72 The laws concerning capital punishment are continu-
73 ally under discussion. Perhaps in the future other states
74 will change their laws, as Indiana did. In the meantime,
75 though, the controversy continues.

• A. Fact-Finding Exercise

Read the passage again. Read the following statements. Check whether they are True (T) or False (F). If a statement is false, rewrite the statement so that it is true. Then go back to the passage and find the line that supports your answer.

_____ T _____ F 1. People may be executed in the United States for committing murder.

____

_____ T _____ F 2. All states in the United States allow the death penalty for serious crimes such as murder.

____

_____ T _____ F 3. South Carolina does not allow capital punishment for minors.

____

_____ T _____ F 4. The governor of a state can stop an execution.

____

_____ T _____ F 5. Americans agree that it is wrong to execute convicted criminals who are minors.

____

_____ T _____ F 6. Opponents of the death penalty believe that capital punishment reduces the number of crimes.

____

_____ T _____ F 7. Proponents of the death penalty believe that capital punishment prevents repeat crimes.

____

• B. Reading Analysis

Read each question carefully. Either circle the letter of the correct answer, or write your answer in the space provided.

1. What is the main idea of the passage?

   a. In the United States, many states allow the death penalty for minors.
   b. Indiana allows the death penalty for minors over the age of 16.
   c. The death penalty for minors is a controversial issue in the United States.

2. In lines 1–3, what is another expression for **capital punishment**?

   a. death penalty
   b. convicted criminal
   c. convicted minor

3. In line 4, what is the purpose of the colon (:)?

   a. to give a definition
   b. to introduce the question
   c. to give more information

4. a. In line 7, what is a **minor**?

   ____

   b. How do you know?

   ____

5. In line 24, what does **while** mean?

   a. but
   b. before
   c. when

6. In line 26, what does **nonetheless** mean?

   a. however
   b. also
   c. instead

7. Read lines 38–41: "Cooper's lawyer appealed to the governor of Indiana to stop the execution. . . ." What does this statement mean?

   a. The lawyer fought with the governor.
   b. The lawyer asked the governor for help.
   c. The lawyer disagreed with the governor.

8. Read lines 42–43: ". . . he had to let the courts do their job." This statement means that

   a. he will stop the execution
   b. he will speak to the court
   c. he will allow the execution

9. Read lines 48–51: "In 1988 the U.S. Supreme Court decided to **bar**, or prohibit, the execution of **juveniles** who were **under the age of 16** when they committed their crime."

   a. **Juveniles** are

      1. minors
      2. young people
      3. children up to age 16

   b. In this sentence, **bar** means

      1. a place to buy wine or beer
      2. prohibit or stop
      3. allow

   c. **under the age of 16** means

      1. younger than 16
      2. older than 16
      3. with 16 people

   d. This sentence means that the Supreme Court said

      1. you cannot execute any minors
      2. you cannot execute minors less than 16 years old
      3. you cannot execute anyone who commits a crime

10. In lines 60–61, what are **opponents**?

    a. people who agree with an issue
    b. people who disagree with an issue
    c. reasons to disagree with an issue

11. In line 68, what are **proponents**?

    a. people who agree with an issue
    b. people who disagree with an issue
    c. reasons to disagree with an issue

12. In line 70, what does **that is** indicate?

    a. an example
    b. a contrast
    c. an explanation

• C. Information Organization

Read the passage again. Underline what you think are the main ideas. Then scan the reading and complete the following chart, using the sentences that you have underlined to help you. You will use this chart later to answer questions about the reading.

MAIN IDEA:	
______ STATES ALLOW CAPITAL PUNISHMENT	
______ STATES PERMIT THE EXECUTION OF MINORS	
SUPREME COURT RULING:	
EXAMPLES OF JUVENILE CRIMINALS	
WHO: AGE: CRIME: PLACE: SENTENCE: APPEALS: RESULT:	WHO: AGE: CRIME: PLACE: SENTENCE: APPEALS: SUPREME COURT RULING: RESULT:
ARGUMENTS FOR AND AGAINST THE DEATH PENALTY	
ARGUMENTS FOR:	ARGUMENTS AGAINST:
1. 2. 3.	1. 2. 3. 4.

• D. Information Recall and Summary

Read each question carefully. Use your chart to answer the questions. Do not refer back to the passage. When you are finished, write a brief summary of the reading.

1. a. Who makes the laws about the death penalty in the United States?

   ____

   b. How many states currently allow capital punishment for minors?

   ____

2. The third paragraph describes a man who was sentenced to death for murder.

   a. Did his lawyer agree with this decision? Why or why not?

   ____

   b. What did the lawyer do to try to change the decision?

   ____

   c. What happened? Was the lawyer successful?

   ____

3. In the United States, who can stop a death sentence? How?

   ____

4. a. In the fourth paragraph, why was the girl sentenced to die?

   ____

   b. Did her lawyer agree with this decision? Why or why not?

   ____

   c. Did the Indiana governor agree with this execution? Why or why not?

   ____

5. a. What did the Supreme Court decide in 1988?

   ____

   b. What happened to Paula Cooper?

   ____

6. What are three arguments for capital punishment?

   a. ____________________

   b. ____________________

   c. ____________________

7. What are four arguments against capital punishment?

   a. ____________________

   b. ____________________

   c. ____________________

   d. ____________________

Summary

Work in pairs or alone. Write a brief summary of the reading, and put it on the blackboard. Compare your summary with your classmates'. Which one best describes the main idea of the reading?

____

____

____

____

• E. Word Forms

Part 1

In English, the noun and verb forms of some words are the same—for example, *murder* (v.) and *murder* (n.).

Complete each sentence with the correct form of the word on the left. **Use the correct tense of the verb in either the affirmative or the negative form. Use the singular or plural form of the noun. In addition, indicate whether you are using the noun (n.) or verb (v.) form.**

limit

1. a. There is no ___________ *(n., v.)* to the number of cars on the road.

   b. The state laws ___________ *(n., v.)* the speed at which motorists are permitted to drive.

appeal

2. a. The lawyer ___________ *(n., v.)* to a higher court next week.

   b. He will make a formal ___________ *(n., v.)* for a lighter sentence.

fear

3. a. Jack believes that ___________ *(n., v.)* is our worst enemy.

   b. We ___________ *(n., v.)* the things we understand; we are afraid only of the things we don't know.

sentence

4. a. The convicted man received a 25-year ___________ *(n., v.)*.

   b. The judge in charge of the case ___________ *(n., v.)* him to 25 years in prison for armed robbery.

change

5. a. Fay ___________ *(n., v.)* her job until she graduates in May.

   b. After graduation, she plans to make a few additional ___________ *(n., v.)* in her life.

Part 2

In English, verbs change to nouns in several ways. Some verbs become nouns by adding the suffix *-ion* or *-ation*—for example, *electrocute* (v.) becomes *electrocution* (n.).

Complete each sentence with the correct form of the words on the left. **Use the correct tense of the verb in either the affirmative or the negative form. Use the singular or plural form of the noun.**

execute (v.)
execution (n.)

1. a. The state __________ the criminal even though he was convicted of murder.
   b. This state has eliminated the ________ of convicted murderers.

convict (v.)
conviction (n.)

2. a. Yesterday, the jury __________ the young man of robbery.
   b. The judge was satisfied with his __________________.

protect (v.)
protection (n.)

3. a. Many people are concerned with the _________ of their homes.
   b. Some people _________ their homes with alarm systems.

suggest (v.)
suggestion (n.)

4. a. Barbara made several wonderful ________ at the meeting last week.
   b. However, she _________ that the office close on Friday, although it is a good idea.

continue (v.)
continuation (n.)

5. a. The generals __________ the battle in the morning.
   b. They believe that the __________ of the fight means they can win the war.

• F. Dictionary Skills

Read the following sentences. Use the context to help you understand the boldface words. Read the dictionary entry for that word and choose the appropriate definition. Then rewrite the sentence, using the definition you have chosen. Be sure to make your sentence grammatically correct.

1. The death penalty for minors is a very serious **issue.** Many people dis agree with it, but others favor it.

issue *n* — **1 a** outgoing; outflowing. **b** the act of flowing out; that which flows out: *an ~ of blood.* **2** putting out; distributing. **3** publication: *the most recent ~s of a periodical.* **4** question that arises for discussion: *to argue political ~s.*

____

2. The governor of each state has the **power** to change a death sentence to life in prison.

power *n* — **1** ability to do or act: *I will do everything in my ~ to help.* **2** strength; force. **3** energy or force that can be used to do work: *electric ~.* **4** control; authority: *the ~ of the law.* **5** legal authority or right: *The President has exceeded his ~.*

____

3. Paula Cooper's lawyer decided to **appeal** to the governor of Indiana in order to stop Cooper's execution.

appeal *v* — **1** make an earnest request: *The prisoner ~ed to the judge for mercy.* **2** (*legal*) take a case to a higher court for review. **3** attract; move the feelings of: *Do these paintings ~ to you?*

____

4. Some people feel that it is wrong to **treat** minors as adults in murder cases.

treat *v* — **1** act or behave toward: *He ~s his wife badly.* **2** consider: *We had better ~ it as a joke,* instead of taking it seriously. **3** discuss; deal with. **4** give medical or surgical care to. **5** put (a substance) through a process (in manufacture, etc.). **6** supply (food, drink, entertainment, etc.) at one's own expense (to): *I will ~ myself/you to a good weekend vacation.*

____

• G. Vocabulary in Context

convicted (v.)
criminal (n.)
currently (adv.)
execute (v.)
limit (n.)
minors (n.)
nonetheless (adv.)
perhaps (adv.)
refused (v.)
surprisingly (adv.)

Read the following sentences. Complete each blank space with the correct word from the list above. Use each word only once.

1. You must be at least 21 years old to drink alcohol in New York, but the age __________ is not the same in every state.

2. In the United States, it is illegal for __________ under the age of 18 to vote.

3. Joanne flew to California on vacation last week. __________, she met an old friend on the plane.

4. __________, Frank is an English student. When he finishes studying English, he will study computer science.

5. My house was robbed last week. The police are looking for the __________ who committed the crime.

6. Jodi was very sick yesterday. __________, she went to work and stayed all day.

7. I can't find my umbrella. __________ I left it on the bus.

8. Paul asked Suzie to marry him, but she __________. She told him that she loved someone else.

9. Many countries __________ convicted murderers, but other countries sentence them to life in prison instead.

10. The court __________ Harriet of stealing a car. A witness said he saw her do it, and the car was found in her garage.

• H. Topics for Discussion and Writing

1. The girl who committed murder at the age of 15 was going to be executed. In 1989, her sentence was changed to 60 years in prison. Do you agree with this sentence? Why or why not?
2. Do you think it is right to treat minors the same as adults in cases of murder? Why or why not?
3. Do you believe in the death penalty? Why or why not?
4. In the United States, 36 states allow capital punishment. Do you think all states should have the same laws, or do you think it is better for each state to make its own decision? Why?

• I. Follow-Up Activities

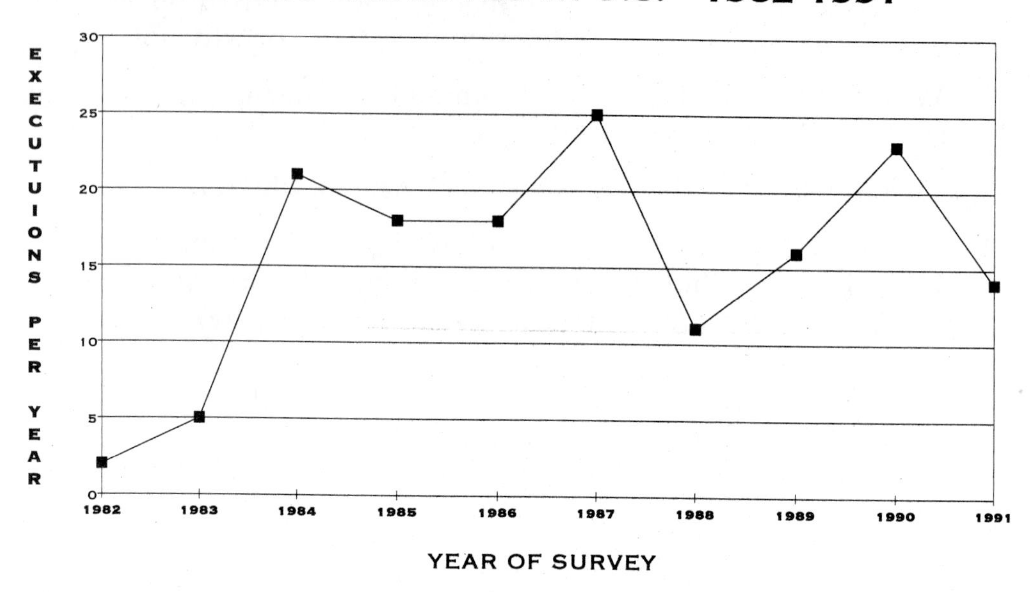

1. Refer to the **Prisoners Executed In the United States 1982–1991** line graph, and answer the following questions.

   a. How many prisoners were executed in 1991?

   ____

   b. What year had the largest number of executions?

   ____

   c. What year had the smallest number of executions?

   ____

   d. Between which two years was there the greatest increase in the number of executions?

   ____

   e. Between which two years was there the greatest decrease in the number of executions?

   ____

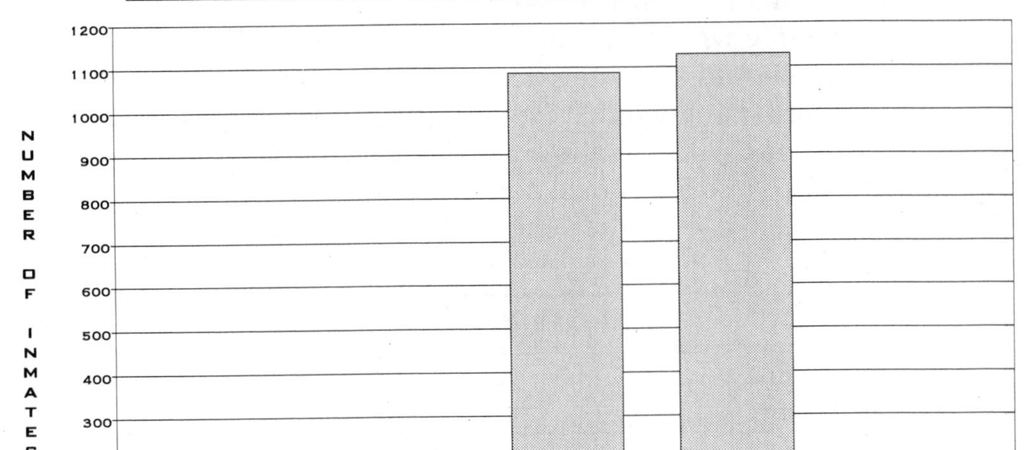

2. Refer to the **U.S. Prisoners Under Sentence of Death—1991** bar graph, and answer the following questions.

   a. In 1991, which age group had the highest number of prisoners under sentence of death?

   ____

   b. Which age group had the smallest number of prisoners under sentence of death?

   ____

   c. Approximately how many prisoners under sentence of death were 20–24 years old?

   ____

   d. Approximately how many prisoners under sentence of death were over 55 years old?

   ____

   e. What reasons might explain the low number of very young and very old prisoners under sentence of death?

   ____

3. Work in a small group with your classmates. Pretend that you are the people who make the laws in your state. Do you think your state should allow the death penalty? Discuss your reasons for (pros) and against (cons) capital punishment. What about minors? Will you allow the death penalty for them? After you discuss your decisions, complete the following chart.

Death Penalty	
Pros	Cons
1.	1.
2.	2.
3.	3.
Death Penalty for Minors:	
Final Decision:	

4. a. Read the Death Penalty Survey on page 145. Go outside your class alone or in pairs. Survey two or three people.

   b. Bring back your data and combine it with the other students' information. Create a bar graph or other chart to display your data. Divide your responses into two groups: those people in favor of the death penalty and those opposed to the death penalty.

   c. Compare your responses with other students responses. How are they similar? How are they different?

Death Penalty Survey

The purpose of this questionnaire is to collect information regarding people's opinions on capital punishment.

Informant is _______ Male _______ Female

Informant is _______ under 20 _______ 40–50

_______ 20–30 _______ over 50

_______ 30–40

Please answer the following questions.

1. What is your opinion on the death penalty?

   _______ in favor _______ not sure

   _______ opposed _______ it depends

2. If you are in favor of the death penalty, what are your reasons?

   _______ It is an appropriate punishment for murder.

   _______ It helps discourage people from committing murder.

   _______ Other

3. If you are opposed to the death penalty, what are your reasons?

   _______ Killing is wrong, even as punishment for murder.

   _______ The death penalty does not discourage people from committing murder.

   _______ If the court makes a mistake, it will be too late to save an innocent person.

   _______ Other

4. If you think it depends on the circumstances, please explain.

   ____

Unit III Review

• J. Crossword Puzzle

Clues

Across

3. Man, woman, ___, girl
4. A ___ is the person a crime is committed against.
7. There are different types of ___ for a crime: prison, fines, and probation.
9. Electrocution and hanging are forms of ___.
10. If a person is proven ___, he or she is convicted.
13. the past of *sit*
14. An ___ is a person who is against something.
16. the opposite of *fail* (a course)
18. We ___ read English well.
19. however: nevertheless
20. An error is a ___.
21. The judge needs some ___, or proof, to show that a suspect really committed a crime.
22. dependability
24. a formal request to a judge for a change in sentence
28. not guilty
29. The basis of something is its ___.
31. Laws are made to protect the ___ rights of all people.

Down

1. A ___ is a person who saw a crime take place.
2. These shoes are the correct size. They ___ me very well.
3. ___ is money the suspect gives the court to ensure that he or she will appear in court again.
5. she, ___, it
6. I will meet you ___ six o'clock.
7. A ___ is a person in favor of something.
8. A ___ is the punishment that the judge gives a convicted person.
10. We will ___ home after class.
11. During a trial, people give ___. They say what they saw or know about the case.
12. one time
15. bar; not allow
16. sure; certain
17. accuse
18. as a result
23. We are going ___ go to the library after class.
24. If a suspect cannot afford a lawyer, the judge may ___ one.
25. the opposite of *first*
26. The police record the charges against a suspect at the police station. They ___ the suspect.
27. ___ , two, three
30. the past of *dive*

• K. Unit III Discussion

The three chapters in this unit all discuss an aspect of crime. Chapter 7 outlines how a suspect is arrested and charged with a crime. Chapter 8 describes how an innocent man was convicted as a result of eyewitnesses' mistakes. Chapter 9 discusses the death penalty and people's conflicting opinions on the death penalty for minors. Should lawmakers and the courts consider such factors as a criminal's home life, age, and physical condition when making laws and punishing convicted criminals? Can courts ensure that eyewitnesses have not made mistakes? If so, how?

Unit IV

Science and History

C·H·A·P·T·E·R 10

Ancient Artifacts and Ancient Air

• Prereading Preparation

1. What kind of work do archeologists perform?
2. What do archeologists study in order to learn about the past?
3. What can archeological discoveries tell us about the past?
4. Where would you find ancient air?
5. How can ancient air help us learn about the past? About the future?

1 Archeologists made an exciting discovery in Egypt in
2 1954. During an excavation near the base of the Great
3 Pyramid, they uncovered an ancient crypt. Although
4 they believed that this discovery would help us under-
5 stand Egypt's past, they also hoped that it would give us
6 important information about the future.
7 This crypt was a tomb, or burial place, for a dead
8 Egyptian pharaoh, or king. Historians believed that the
9 Egyptians buried their pharaohs with two boats: one to
10 carry the body and the other to carry the soul. This was
11 one of their religious customs about death. The arche-
12 ologists expected to find two boats inside the crypt. As
13 they broke the crypt open, they smelled the scent of
14 wood. The ancient Egyptians had sealed the room so ef-
15 fectively that the aroma of the cedar wood was still pre-
16 served. Inside the crypt, archeologists found a
17 4,600-year-old boat that was in almost perfect condi-
18 tion. In addition, they found another closed room next
19 to the crypt. Archeologists and historians believed that
20 this chamber contained the second boat. If so, archeolo-
21 gists would have better information about the past.
22 They would be sure about the religious custom of bury-
23 ing pharaohs with two boats.
24 However, this was not the only information they
25 hoped to find. They wondered if the air in the two

rooms contained something special that helped to preserve the wood. This information could help in the preservation of ancient artifacts in museums throughout the world. Researchers also hoped to find some answers about the future by carefully examining the air in the second chamber. When the archeologists opened the first chamber, all the old air escaped. Scientists wanted to recover the air in the second chamber, compare it with the air of the present, and then examine the differences, especially differences in the level of carbon dioxide (CO_2). This information might help them predict changes in the air in the future. They also did not want outside air to get inside the chamber. Careful planning would be necessary in order to open the second room and save the air. In fact, it took years to plan the excavation and to design and make the equipment necessary to open the chamber and collect the air inside.

Finally, in October 1986 an international team of scientists, using special equipment, drilled through the roof of the chamber. The hole they made was kept carefully sealed. As they broke into the ancient room, they realized that the chamber was not sealed. They took an air sample. The air inside was the same as the air outside. The scientists were very disappointed. However, they continued working to see what was inside the chamber. The team lowered a light and a camera into the small hole, and looked at the interior of the room on a television monitor. The second boat was really there!

After the scientists took samples of the air inside the chamber and photographed it completely, they sealed up the hole in the roof and left the room as they had found it. Although they did not get samples of 4,600-year-old air, they did confirm the Egyptian custom of burying pharaohs with two boats. More importantly, they practiced a new, nondestructive approach to archeology: investigate an ancient location, photograph it, and leave it untouched. When archeologists opened the first chamber, they removed the boat. The Egyptian government built a museum on the site for the first boat. During the construction of the museum, the vibrations from the heavy machinery disturbed the second room and probably destroyed the seal. Water leaked in, too, so the second boat was not as well preserved as the first boat.

70 The investigation of the second chamber taught ar-
71 cheologists a valuable lesson. New excavations will not
72 only use modern technology, but they will also follow
73 the idea of preserving the entire location for future
74 studies.

• A. Fact-Finding Exercise

Read the passage again. Read the following statements. Check whether they are True (T) or False (F). If a statement is false, rewrite the statement so that it is true. Then go back to the passage and find the line that supports your answer.

_____ T _____ F 1. Archeological discoveries give us information about the past.

____

_____ T _____ F 2. Archeologists recently discovered a body in a crypt in Egypt.

____

_____ T _____ F 3. Archeologists found a boat in the second crypt near the Great Pyramids.

____

_____ T _____ F 4. Archeologists have not opened the second room yet.

____

_____ T _____ F 5. There is no old air left in the second chamber.

____

_____ T _____ F 6. The investigation team went inside the second chamber.

____

_____ T _____ F 7. The Egyptian government is going to put the second boat in a museum.

____

• B. Reading Analysis

Read each question carefully. Either circle the letter of the correct answer, or write your answer in the space provided.

1. What is the main idea of the passage?
   a. Analyzing old air is important because it helps us understand the future and preserve ancient artifacts.
   b. A recent archeological discovery helped us understand the future and the past, and introduced new technology.
   c. Archeologists recently discovered a crypt near the Great Pyramid in Egypt, and they carefully examined it.
2. In line 3, what is the purpose of **although**?
   a. It introduces two different ideas.
   b. It introduces two similar ideas.
   c. It introduces two new ideas.
3. In line 7, what is a **crypt**?

   ____
4. In line 8, what is a synonym for **pharaoh**?

   ____
5. Read lines 8–10. What is the purpose of the colon (:)?
   a. It shows that the sentence continues for another line.
   b. It connects two sentences and makes them one sentence.
   c. It introduces the purpose of the two boats.

6. In line 12, what does **as** mean?

   a. before
   b. like
   c. when

7. In line 14, what does **sealed** mean?

   a. locked with a key
   b. closed completely
   c. hidden carefully

8. Read lines 16–21.

   a. What comes after **in addition**?

      1. more information
      2. the same information
      3. the result of the previous information

   b. What does **chamber** mean?

      1. crypt
      2. room
      3. historian

   c. What does **if so** mean?

      1. if the second chamber really contained a second boat
      2. if archeologists could be sure of the Egyptian custom
      3. if there was really a second chamber next to the crypt

9. In line 24, why is **however** used at the beginning of the paragraph?

   a. to show that the paragraph gives the same information as the paragraph before it
   b. to show that the paragraph gives different information from the paragraph before it

10. Read lines 32–36.

    a. What does $\mathbf{CO_2}$ represent?

       1. an abbreviation
       2. an amount
       3. a chemical symbol

    b. What is $\mathbf{CO_2}$?

    ____

    c. How do you know?

    ____

11. Read lines 38–42. What is the purpose of **in fact**?

    a. to give true information
    b. to emphasize the previous information
    c. to introduce different information

12. Read lines 57–59.

    a. What is the purpose of **did** in line 58?
        1. to form a question
        2. to show the past
        3. to give emphasis

    b. What does **confirm** mean?

        1. see
        2. prove
        3. write

13. Read lines 60–62. What is the purpose of the colon (:)?

    a. It shows that the sentence continues for another line.
    b. It connects two sentences and makes them one sentence.
    c. It introduces the new nondestructive approach to archeology.

14. Read lines 71–74: "New excavations will not only use modern technology, but they will also follow the idea of preserving the entire location for future studies." What is a synonym for **not only . . . but also**?

    a. and
    b. but
    c. so

• C. Information Organization

Read the passage again. Underline what you think are the main ideas. Then scan the reading and complete the following outline, using the sentences that you have underlined to help you. You will use this outline later to answer questions about the reading.

I. Archeological Discovery in Egypt

   A. Date:
   B. Place:
   C. The Discovery:

II. Historians' Belief About Egyptian Burial Customs

   A.
   B. The Purpose of the Boats:

III. The Excavation of the Crypt

   A.
   B.
   C.

IV. What the Archeologists and Historians Hoped to Learn

   A. Information about the Past:
   B. Information about Preserving Wood:
   C. Information about the Future:

V. The Excavation of the Second Chamber

   A. Date:
   B. Method of Excavation:
      1.
      2.
      3.
      4.

VI. The Significance of the Second Excavation

   A.
   B. They practiced a new, nondestructive approach to archeology:
      1.
      2.
      3.
   C. They found out that when the Egyptian government built a museum for the first boat, vibrations from the machinery disturbed the second room and destroyed the seal.

• D. Information Recall and Summary

Read each question carefully. Use your outline to answer the questions. Do not refer back to the passage. When you are finished, write a brief summary of the reading.

1. Where and when did archeologists discover the crypt?

   ____

2. What was the purpose of the crypt?

   ____

3. What is an ancient Egyptian religious custom about death?

   ____

4. Why was the second chamber so important to historians?

   ____

5. How did researchers hope to find answers about the future in the second chamber?

   ____

6. a. Why did it take such a long time before the team opened the second chamber?

   ____

   b. How was the excavation of the second chamber different from the excavation of the first chamber?

   ____

7. How did the air in the second chamber escape?

   ____

   ____

8. What did the team do after they opened and photographed the second chamber?

   ____

Summary

Work in pairs or alone. Write a brief summary of the reading, and put it on the blackboard. Compare your summary with your classmates'. Which one best describes the main idea of the reading?

____

____

____

• E. Word Forms

Part 1

In English, verbs change to nouns in several ways. Some verbs become nouns by adding the suffix *-ion* or *-ation* —for example, *preserve* (v.) becomes *preservation* (n.).

Complete each sentence with the correct form of the words on the left. **Use the correct tense of the verb in either the affirmative or the negative form. Use the singular or plural form of the noun.**

predict (v.) prediction (n.)	1. a. The weather forecast ________ snow for last night, but it snowed anyway. b. The ________ about the weather was incorrect.
correct (v.) correction (n.)	2. a. After our teacher assigns an essay, he always ________ the papers. b. If there are only a few ________, the students get good grades.
excavate (v.) excavation (n.)	3. a. The ________ of King Tut's tomb was an important and famous event. b. Archeologists ________ this tomb in Egypt in the 1920s.
examine (v.) examination (n.)	4. a. The doctor's ________ of the sick child will take a long time. b. The doctor ________ the sick child until tomorrow to find out what is wrong.
inform (v.) information (n.)	5. a. The teacher ________ us about the TOEFL right now. b. This ________ will be very helpful to all of us.

Part 2

In English, verbs change to nouns in several ways. Some verbs become nouns by adding the suffix *-y*—for example, *embroider* (v.) becomes *embroidery* (n.).

Complete each sentence with the correct form of the words on the left. **Use the correct tense of the verb in either the affirmative or the negative form. Use the singular or plural form of the noun.**

recover (v.)
recovery (n.)

1. a. Everyone was amazed at the old man's ____________.
   b. The doctor really thought he was going to die, but he ____________ completely.

discover (v.)
discovery (n.)

2. a. An important ________ that may take place soon is the cure for cancer.
   b. Researchers ________ a cure for cancer in the near future.

deliver (v.)
delivery (n.)

3. a. The letter carrier ____________ the mail early every morning. She comes in the afternoon.
   b. I am excited about the ________ because I am waiting for a letter from my mother.

inquire (v.)
inquiry (n.)

4. a. When Marla arrived at the airport, she ____________ about flights to Paris and to London.
   b. Marla made both ________ at the Information Desk.

master (v.)
mastery (n.)

5. a. After studying English for four years, Angela finally __________ the language.
   b. Her ____________ of English helped her get a higher-paying job.

• F. Dictionary Skills

Read the following sentences. Use the context to help you understand the boldface words. Read the dictionary entry for that word and choose the appropriate definition. Then rewrite the sentence, using the definition you have chosen. Be sure to make your sentence grammatically correct.

1. In 1954, archeologists uncovered an ancient crypt near the **base** of the Great Pyramid.

base *n* — **1** lowest part of anything, esp. the part on which a thing rests or is supported; foundation. **2** place at which armed forces, expeditions, etc. have their stores, hospitals, etc. **3** (*geometry*) line or surface on that a figure stands or can stand. **4** (*math*) the number (usually 10) that is the starting point for a numerical system.

___

2. The ancient Egyptians had a religious **custom.** They buried their pha raohs with two boats: one to carry the body and the other to carry the soul.

custom *n* — **1** usual and generally accepted behavior or practice among members of a social group; tradition. **2** particular way of behaving; habit: *Social ~s vary in different countries.* **3** regular business given to a firm by its customers. **4** taxes due to the government on goods imported into a country; import duties.

___

3. The air **escaped** from the second chamber at the time the museum was built for the first boat.

escape *v* — **1** get free; get away: *Two prisoners have ~d.* **2** find a way out; leak: *The gas has ~d from this hole.* **3** avoid; keep free or safe from: *You were lucky to ~ punishment.* **4** be forgotten or unnoticed by: *His name ~s me for the moment.*

___

4. The scientists **lowered** a light and a camera into the second chamber.

lower *v* — **1** let or bring down: *~ the sails/a flag.* **2** make or become less in value, amount, etc.: *~ the rent of a house.* **3** drop, become less in volume: *She ~ed her voice to a whisper.*

___

• G. Vocabulary in Context

although (conj.)
custom (n.)
discovered (v.)
excavation (n.)
if so
in addition
in fact
predict (v.)
recover (v.)
sealed (adj.)

Read the following sentences. Complete each blank space with the correct word or phrase from the list above. Use each word or phrase only once.

1. ________ I am sick, I can't stay home. I have to go to work anyway.

2. Debbie is doing very well in college. ________, she got 100% on her last five tests and an A+ on her research paper.

3. In the United States, it is a ________ for people to shake hands when they first meet.

4. Today, bottles and cans in stores are carefully ________ to prevent air and germs from getting inside.

5. The supermarket may be open late tonight. ________, I will go shopping after work instead of early tomorrow morning.

6. During the ________ of an old building, construction workers found some ancient artifacts.

7. English students must study grammar. ________, they must study reading, writing, and listening comprehension.

8. Tommy left his sweater in the cafeteria. Fortunately, he was able to ________ it at the Lost and Found Office.

9. Some people go to fortune tellers, who use cards in order to ________ what the future will be.

10. Christopher Columbus ________ America in 1492. Before Columbus found America, most people did not know about its existence.

• H. Topics for Discussion and Writing

1. a. How do archeological discoveries help us understand the past?

   b. Why is understanding the past important?

2. How can the analysis of ancient air be important?

3. a. Do you think it is important not to disturb ancient locations? Why or why not?

   b. Are there times when it is better to remove ancient artifacts and take them to a museum? When?

4. The archeological team left the second boat in the chamber and sealed it again. Do you think it would be better to put the second boat in a museum, too? Why or why not?

• I. Follow-Up Activity

In groups of three or four, form a panel of experts. Someone has discovered the ruins of an ancient city in your country. Your government wants to investigate this site and has asked your panel to plan the excavation. In your group, decide who you will need to help you with this project. Plan the work that your group will do at this location. Decide which artifacts you will take away to a museum and which ones you will leave at the site. When you are finished, compare your plan with your classmates' plans. As a class, decide which plan the government should use.

C·H·A·P·T·E·R 11

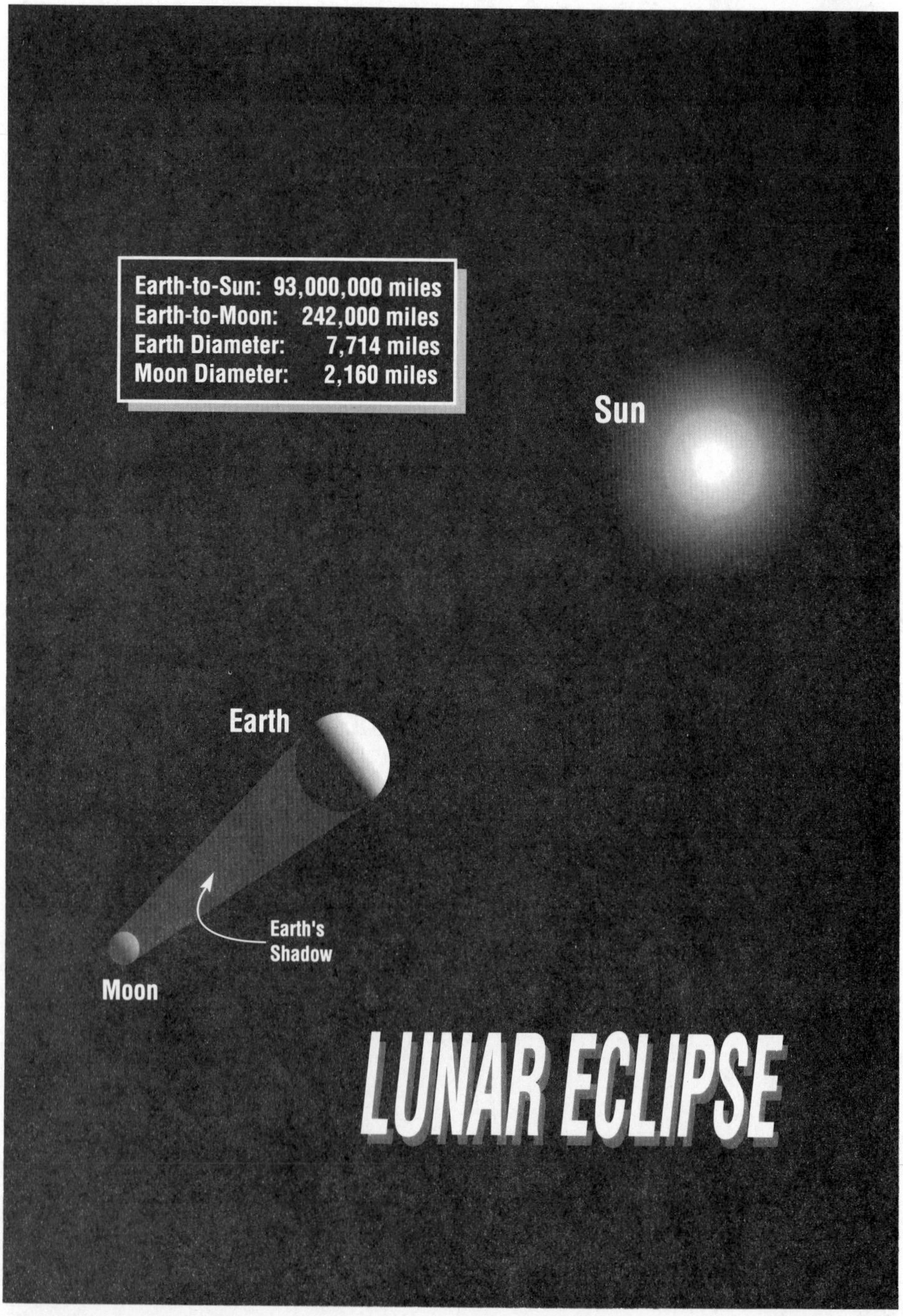

Earth-to-Sun: 93,000,000 miles
Earth-to-Moon: 242,000 miles
Earth Diameter: 7,714 miles
Moon Diameter: 2,160 miles

Sun

Earth

Earth's Shadow

Moon

LUNAR ECLIPSE

How Lunar Eclipses Have Changed History

• Prereading Preparation

1. Refer to the illustration on the left. Describe a lunar eclipse.
2. Have you ever seen a lunar eclipse? How does the sky look during a lunar eclipse? What color does the moon appear to be?
3. In the past, some people were superstitious about eclipses. What do you think they believed? Why do you think they were afraid?

Lunar eclipses have always fascinated people. Some study eclipses as an astronomical phenomenon; others just enjoy observing their beauty. However, in ancient—and even in more recent—times, lunar eclipses were mysterious, unpredictable, and frightening. In the past, people believed that eclipses were bad omens, or signs, and this superstition has often affected historical events. For instance, a lunar eclipse was partly responsible for the fall of Constantinople in 1453.

Constantinople was named for the Roman emperor Constantine, who moved his capital to Byzantium (present-day Istanbul in Turkey) in 324 A.D. The Byzantine government ruled the area for over a thousand years.

In the 15th century, the Ottoman (Turkish) Empire was planning to take over Constantinople. The Turkish troops attacked Constantinople in 1402 and again in 1422, but did not succeed. Then in 1451, sultan Mohammed II attacked the city again. Mohammed II had several advantages over the defenders of the city. For instance, he had 250,000 men in his army; Constantinople was fortified by only 7,000 troops. The sultan also had a new style of cannon that shot stones that weighed 1,300 pounds. This weapon was capable of breaking through Constantinople's thick walls. In April

1453, the Turkish army attacked the city's thick walls with its new cannon. The defenders, however, repaired the walls every night. Furthermore, they attacked back several times. Still, after some time, the 7,000 defenders became exhausted. They never thought of giving up, however, because they had faith in an old prophecy. The prediction stated that Constantinople could never fall while the moon was becoming full. Unfortunately, on May 22, 1453, the full moon went into an eclipse. The defenders felt frightened and helpless. Three days later, Mohammed II attacked the city again. In a very short time, the Turkish army overpowered Constantinople's troops. Constantinople's defenders had believed the evil omen about the moon; the lunar eclipse made them feel that the battle would be hopeless, and they lost their ability to protect their city from the enemy.

A lunar eclipse affected the course of history in Asia, too. According to an ancient Chinese maxim, or saying, each Chinese dynasty starts out when the previous dynasty becomes corrupt, i.e., immoral. This principle is called the Mandate of Heaven because signs in the sky will show that the emperor has become unworthy to rule. The Manchu (Ch'ing) Dynasty in China began its rule in 1644. At first the dynasty was a glorious one, but by the mid 1800s it had become very corrupt. Finally, in 1851, the Taiping Rebellion took place in order to overthrow the Manchu Dynasty. Some Western powers helped the Manchus try to remain in power. The Manchus also received help from an army of mercenary[1] soldiers. A British officer named Charles Gordon was a very successful leader of this mercenary army.

The rebels were defending the city of Soochow, and Gordon's forces were beating them. The rebels' final defense was at the east gate of the city. Gordon decided to make a night attack because there was a full moon and his troops would have enough light to see by. Unfortunately, on the night he chose for his assault there was a lunar eclipse. The Chinese mercenaries interpreted the eclipse as an evil omen, based on the Mandate of Heaven, and felt defeated even before they began to fight. The attack on Soochow was unsuccessful, and a

[1] Mercenaries are men who make money by hiring themselves out as soldiers to anyone who is willing to pay them. They are also called *soldiers of fortune*.

large number of the mercenary soldiers were killed. This battle was Gordon's only loss. Although the mercenaries were unable to take Shoochow, the Taiping Rebellion failed, and the Manchu Dynasty remained in power.

Today, scientists can predict lunar eclipses. We no longer fear them as evil omens. However, it is not difficult to understand how, in the past, people believed that eclipses were signs of disaster because they did not understand their true cause.

• A. Fact-Finding Exercise

Read the passage again. Read the following statements. Check whether they are True (T) or False (F). If a statement is false, rewrite the statement so that it is true. Then go back to the passage and find the line that supports your answer.

_____ T _____ F 1. Many people today think that eclipses are bad signs.

____

_____ T _____ F 2. Constantinople's defenders failed partly because they thought the eclipse was a bad omen.

____

_____ T _____ F 3. In 1851 the Taiping Rebellion overthrew the Manchu Dynasty.

____

_____ T _____ F 4. Gordon decided to make a night attack against Soochow because there was an eclipse.

____

_____ T _____ F 5. Scientists know when lunar eclipses will occur.

____

• B. Reading Analysis

Read each question carefully. Either circle the letter of the correct answer, or write your answer in the space provided.

1. What is the main idea of the passage?
   a. Scientists today can predict lunar eclipses, so people are not afraid of them anymore.
   b. History was affected because people in the past thought lunar eclipses were evil omens.
   c. In 1453, the Turkish army overpowered Constantinople's defenders, and the city fell.
2. In lines 3–4, what is between the dashes (—)?
   a. an example
   b. more information
   c. an explanation

3. Read lines 5–8.

   a. In line 6, what is another word for **omen**?

   ____

   b. How do you know?

   ____

   c. In line 7, what is **this superstition**?

   ____

4. a. Read lines 10–12. What is the name of **Byzantium** today?

   ____

   b. How do you know?

   ____

5. Read lines 12–14: "The Byzantine government ruled the area for over a thousand years."

   a. In this sentence, **ruled** means

      1. fought
      2. governed
      3. defended

   b. In this sentence, **over** means

      1. about
      2. more than
      3. above

6. Read lines 20–22. What does **for instance** mean?

   a. for example
   b. as a result
   c. therefore

7. a. In line 28, what follows **furthermore**?

      1. more information
      2. examples
      3. an explanation

   b. Complete the following sentence:
   Carol is going to be very busy this summer because she is moving into a new house. Furthermore,

      1. she recently got a new job and must travel a lot for her company.
      2. it is very hot in the summer and she does not like the heat.
      3. she has many friends who are going to help her.

8. a. In line 29, what does **still** mean?

   1. in addition
   2. even so
   3. not moving

   b. Complete the following sentence:
   Kelly is very busy with her family, her home, and her job. Still,

   1. she enjoys her job very much.
   2. she never takes a vacation in the summer.
   3. she always makes time to exercise and eat well.

9. Read lines 30–33. What is a synonym for **prophecy**?

   ____

10. a. In line 33, what follows **unfortunately**?

    1. an example
    2. a bad thing
    3. an unbelievable thing

    b. Complete the following sentence:
    Jordan wanted to wake up early in the morning so that he could study for his exam before class. Unfortunately,

    1. his alarm clock didn't ring and he overslept.
    2. he woke up at 6 A.M.
    3. the test was very easy and he passed it.

11. Read lines 43–48.

    a. In line 43, what is a **maxim**?

    ____

    b. How do you know?

    ____

    c. What does **corrupt** mean?

    ____

    d. How do you know?

    ____

    e. What is the **Mandate of Heaven**?

    ____

    f. Why does it have this name?

    ____

12. In line 50, what period of time is the **mid 1800s**?

    a. 1810–1830
    b. 1840–1860
    c. 1860–1880

13. Read lines 50–53.

    a. What does **overthrow** mean?

       1. replace by force
       2. defend
       3. improve

    b. What are Western **powers**?

       1. forces
       2. strengths
       3. countries

14. a. In lines 54 and 55, what are **mercenary soldiers**?

    ____

    b. How do you know?

    ____

    c. This type of information is called a(n)

       1. index.
       2. footnote.
       3. glossary.

• C. Information Organization

Read the passage again. Underline what you think are the main ideas. Then scan the reading and complete the following chart, using the sentences that you have underlined to help you.You will use this chart later to answer questions about the reading.

Place	*Constantinople*	*China*
Super-stition		
Event and Date		
Result of the Lunar Eclipse		

• D. Information Recall and Summary

Read each question carefully. Use your chart to answer the questions. Do not refer back to the passage. When you are finished, write a brief summary of the reading.

1. What belief did the people of Constantinople have about their city?

 ____

 ____

2. Who attacked Constantinople? When?

 ____

3. a. Who had more men: the defenders of Constantinople, or the attacking army?

 ____

 b. Were the defenders successfully defending their city?

 ____

4. What happened after the full moon went into an eclipse on May 22, 1453?

 ____

 ____

 ____

5. What did the Chinese Mandate of Heaven predict?

 ____

 ____

6. What was the purpose of the Taiping Rebellion?

 ____

 ____

7. Why did Gordon lose his only battle in the rebellion?

 ____

 ____

 ____

Summary

Work in pairs or alone. Write a brief summary of the reading, and put it on the blackboard. Compare your summary with your classmates'. Which one best describes the main idea of the reading?

____

____

____

____

____

• E. Word Forms

Part 1

In English, adjectives change to nouns in several ways. Some adjectives become nouns by adding the suffix *-ity*—for example, *individual* (adj.) becomes *individuality* (n.).

Complete each sentence with the correct form of the words on the left. **Use the singular or plural form of the noun.**

final (adj.)
finality (n.)

1. a. The judge firmly stated that her decision was ______________. She would not change her mind.
   b. She stressed the absolute __________ of her decision by getting up and leaving the courtroom.

unpredictable (adj.)
unpredictability (n.)

2. a. It is a well-known maxim that the weather is always very ______________.
   b. In fact, the only predictable thing about the weather is its ______________.

able (adj.)
ability (n.)

3. a. Jesse has a number of ____________.
   b. For example, he is ___________ to speak three languages, he knows how to build furniture, and he teaches computer science at the college.

responsible (adj.)
responsibility (n.)

4. a. As we grow up, we take on more and more __________, especially if we marry and have children.
   b. We become ___________ for our family, our job, and our home.

capable (adj.)
capability (n.)

5. a. Susan is only three years old. She isn't really _________ of riding a bicycle yet.
   b. Her physical _____________ are still very limited.

Part 2

In English, nouns change to adjectives in several ways. Some nouns become adjectives by adding the suffix *-ous*—for example, *danger* (n.) becomes *dangerous* (adj.).

Complete each sentence with the correct form of the words on the left. **Use the singular or plural form of the noun**.

advantage (n.)
advantageous (adj.)

1. a. Before deciding to study in the United States, Maria made a list of the ________ and disadvantages of going to college in another country.
   b. She decided that it was more __________ to study abroad than at home.

superstition (n.)
superstitious (adj.)

2. a. Jack is the most ___________ person I've ever met. He won't even go into a building that has a 13th floor.
   b. _____________ about lucky and unlucky numbers are cultural. For instance, 13 is not an unlucky number in Japan, but it is in the United States.

mystery (n.)
mysterious (adj.)

3. a. I received a very ____________ package yesterday. When I opened the box, it was empty, and I didn't know who sent it.
   b. I finally solved my little _________ when my sister called and told me she had mailed the box to me.

rebellion (n.)
rebellious (adj.)

4. a. The people in that country are very ____________ because their government is so unjust.
   b. The government has to deal with several ________________ every year, and it isn't succeeding.

disaster (n.)
disastrous (adj.)

5. a. If an earthquake struck our city, it would have ________________ results.
   b. This type of ______________ would cause hundreds of deaths and injuries.

• F. Dictionary Skills

Read the following sentences. Use the context to help you understand the boldface words. Read the dictionary entry for that word and choose the appropriate definition. Then rewrite the sentence, using the definition you have chosen. Be sure to make your sentence grammatically correct.

1. The fall of Constantinople occurred in 1453. This **event** was of great historical significance.

event *n* **1** something (usually important) that happens or has happened; *the chief ~s of 1901.* **2** fact of a thing happening; *in the ~ of his death.* **3** outcome; result. **4** one of the races, competitions, etc. in a sports program.

---

2. An old prophecy predicted that Constantinople could never **fall** while the moon was becoming full.

fall *v* **1** come or go down freely: *He fell into the water.* **2** no longer stand; come to the ground; collapse: *He fell over and broke his leg.* **3** come or go to a lower level or point; become lower or less: *The temperature is ~ing rapidly.* **4** be overcome or defeated; be captured. **5** occur, have as date: *Easter ~s early next year.*

---

3. The Byzantine rulers **ruled** over a large area for over a thousand years.

rule *v* **1** govern; have authority: *Is it true that she tries to ~ the office?* **2** control, guide, or influence: *Don't be ~d by hatred.* **3** give as a decision. **4** make (a line or lines) on paper (with a ruler).

---

4. Lunar eclipses have affected the **course** of history in many countries.

course *n* **1** forward movement in space or time; progress: *the ~ of events.* **2** direction of movement or progress: *The ship is off/ on the right ~.* **3** ground laid out for games: *a golf ~.* **4** series of talks, treatments, etc. **5** one of the several parts of a meal, e.g., soup, fish, dessert: *a five-~dinner; the main ~.*

____

• G. Vocabulary in Context

affects (v.)	failed (v.)	prophecy (n.)
also (adv.)	maxim (n.)	remains (v.)
attacked (v.)	mysterious (adj.)	still (adv.)
disastrous (adj.)		

Read the following sentences. Complete each blank space with the correct word from the list above. Use each word only once.

1. Gloria ________ to understand Mitch's explanation of the math problem, so she asked Ann to explain it.
2. The effects of last week's storm were ____________. Two bridges and 15 buildings were destroyed, and 25 people died.
3. I don't believe the ____________ that you can't teach an old dog new tricks.
4. Jan has been studying Russian for three years, but he ________ doesn't understand it very well.
5. It's really true that the weather strongly ____________ us. We feel very happy on a clear, sunny day, but we feel depressed on a cold, cloudy day.
6. Cynthia studied full-time at the college last semester. She ____________ worked at a full-time job.
7. Our neighbor's dog __________ a burglar in their yard last night. The burglar got away, but he wasn't able to steal anything.
8. I've often heard people tell about the __________ that the world will end, but I don't believe it.
9. Our teacher usually ___________ in the room for several minutes after class has ended to answer our questions.
10. A very ___________ murder took place in town last week. No one knows who the victim was or why he was killed.

• H. Topics for Discussion and Writing

1. Think about a superstition about the sun, planets, and stars that you know about. Describe the superstition and whether it has had good or bad effects on the people/history of your country.

2. Astrologers are people who study the heavens and use the sun, stars, and planets to tell people about their past, present, and future. In a small group, discuss this belief in the effect of the sun, stars, and planets on people's lives. How do you think this belief began?

• I. Follow-Up Activities

1. Even today, many people in different countries have superstitions about the sun, planets, and stars. In small groups, discuss these superstitions in your country and in other countries. Compare your list with your classmates' lists.

Country	Superstitions

2. Most daily newspapers print horoscopes, which predict a person's personality and good or bad luck for that day. Bring a newspaper to class. Each student will read his or her horoscope. Discuss what the horoscope says. Do you believe it? Why or why not? Is the horoscope true for each person with the same "sign?"

3. Solar eclipses (eclipses of the sun) occur throughout the world. Working with a partner, draw an illustration of a solar eclipse. Describe how a solar eclipse takes place.

C·H·A·P·T·E·R 12

Mars: Our Neighbor in Space

• Prereading Preparation

1. What do you know about the planet Mars?
2. Do you think life exists on Mars today? Why or why not?
3. How can we find out if there is life on Mars?
4. What do you think the surface of Mars is like?
5. What do you think the atmosphere of Mars is like?

1 Astronomers all over the world were waiting in ex-
2 citement as August 1993 approached. *Mars Observer*,
3 the American spacecraft, was scheduled to move into
4 orbit around Mars and begin sending new information
5 back to Earth. In addition to mapping the planet, *Mars*
6 *Observer* was going to study the Martian atmosphere
7 and surface. Unfortunately, scientists lost contact with
8 *Mars Observer* on August 24. The *Mars Observer* mis-
9 sion, which cost $845 million, failed.
10 In contrast, the United States' previous mission to
11 Mars was a great success. In 1976, two American space-
12 craft landed on Mars in order to search for signs of life.
13 The tests that the Viking landers performed had nega-
14 tive results. However, scientists still had questions
15 about our close neighbor in space. They wanted to in-
16 vestigate further into the possibility of life on Mars.
17 This was the purpose of the *Mars Observer* mission.
18 Scientists' interest in the Red Planet is based on an
19 assumption. They believe that 4.5 billion years ago,
20 Mars and Earth began their existence under similar con-
21 ditions. During the first billion years, liquid water—in
22 contrast to ice—was abundant on the surface of Mars.
23 This is an indication that Mars was much warmer at that
24 time. Mars also had a thicker atmosphere of carbon di-
25 oxide (CO_2). Many scientists think it is possible that life
26 began under these favorable conditions. After all, Earth

had the same conditions during its first billion years, when life arose. At some point in time, Earth developed an atmosphere that is rich in oxygen, and an ozone layer. Ozone (O_3) is a form of oxygen. The ozone layer protects Earth from harmful ultraviolet light from the sun. While life not only began on Earth, it also survived and became more complex. In contrast, Mars lost its thick atmosphere of carbon dioxide. Ultraviolet radiation intensified. The planet eventually grew colder, and its water froze.

A biologist at NASA (the National Aeronautics and Space Administration), Chris McKay, has suggested three theories about life on Mars. One possibility is that life never developed. A second possibility is that life arose on Mars just as it did on Earth and survived for at least a billion years. The third is that life arose and simple organisms developed. When environmental conditions on Mars changed, life ended.

The two Viking landers performed four experiments. Three experiments tested for biological activity in the soil. However, these tests did not lead to any definite results. The fourth experiment looked for any evidence of life, dead or alive, but found none.

Scientists were dissatisfied with the Viking mission. The two sites where the spacecraft landed provided safe landing places, but they were not particularly interesting locations. Scientists believe there are other areas on Mars that are similar to specific places on Earth that support life. For example, an area in Antarctica, southern Victoria Land, which is not covered by ice, resembles an area on Mars. In the dry valleys of southern Victoria Land, the temperature averages below zero, yet biologists found simple life forms (microorganisms) in rocks and frozen lakes. Perhaps this is also true of places on Mars.

Scientists want another investigation of Mars. They want to map the planet's surface and land a spacecraft in a more promising location. They want to search for fossils, the ancient remains of life. If life ever existed on Mars, scientists believe that future missions might find records of it under sand, or in the ice. They are very disappointed in the failure of the *Mars Observer* mission and want to start a new mission. Other countries are interested in Mars, too. For example, Russia is also plan-

71 ning to send an unmanned spacecraft to Mars sometime
72 before the year 2000.
73 Even if future missions discover no evidence of past
74 or present life on Mars, scientists will look for the an-
75 swers to other, intriguing questions. How is Earth differ-
76 ent from Mars? How can we explain the development of
77 life here on our planet and not on Mars, our close neigh-
78 bor? Are we alone in the universe?

Courtesy of Jet Propulsion Laboratory

• A. Fact-Finding Exercise

Read the passage again. Read the following statements. Check whether they are True (T) or False (F). If a statement is false, rewrite the statement so that it is true. Then go back to the passage and find the line that suports your answer.

_____ T _____ F 1. *Mars Observer* was successful in 1993.

____

_____ T _____ F 2. The 1976 Viking mission to Mars was successful.

____

_____ T _____ F 3. Mars and Earth were very similar 4.5 billion years ago.

____

_____ T _____ F 4. Scientists believe there is liquid water on Mars now.

____

_____ T _____ F 5. The two Viking landers performed three experiments.

____

_____ T _____ F 6. The spacecraft landed at two safe but uninteresting places.

____

_____ T _____ F 7. Scientists believe they may find ancient remains of life on Mars under sand or in ice.

____

_____ T _____ F 8. Russia may send a spacecraft to Mars.

____

• B. Reading Analysis

Read each question carefully. Either circle the letter of the correct answer, or write your answer in the space provided.

1. What is the main idea of the passage?

   a. NASA biologists have three possible theories about life on Mars.
   b. The United States sent two missions to Mars, but one was unsuccessful.
   c. Scientists are interested in the possibility that there is or was life on Mars.

2. The author of this article is in favor of sending more spacecraft to Mars.

   a. yes
   b. no
   c. We don't know.

3. Read lines 5–7.

   a. How many tasks was *Mars Observer* going to perform?

      1. one
      2. two
      3. three

   b. How do you know?

   ____

4. Read lines 8–11.

   a. What does **in contrast** indicate?

      1. two similar ideas
      2. two opposite ideas

   b. Which two words show this relationship?

   ____

5. In line 15, what does **our close neighbor in space** refer to?

   a. the spacecraft
   b. Mars
   c. the sun

6. In line 18, what does **the Red Planet** refer to?

   a. the sun
   b. Earth
   c. Mars

7. Read lines 19–21. Which of the following statements is true?

   a. Mars is older than Earth.
   b. Earth is older than Mars.
   c. Mars and Earth are the same age.

8. Read lines 21–22. "During the first billion years, liquid water—in contrast to ice—was abundant on the surface of Mars."

   a. What form does the water on Mars have today?

      1. liquid
      2. solid

   b. How do you know?

   ____

9. In line 25 and in line 30, what do $C0_2$ and 0_3 represent?

   a. chemical symbols
   b. abbreviations
   c. amounts

10. a. In lines 37 and 38, what is in parentheses?

       1. an abbreviation
       2. the purpose of NASA
       3. the words that NASA stands for

    b. Why do you think **NASA** is used in the sentence, and **National Aeronautics and Space Administration** is in parentheses?

    ____

11. In line 47, what does **definite** indicate?

    a. certainty
    b. uncertainty

12. In lines 50–57, which three words are synonyms of **sites**?

    ____

13. Read lines 57–60. What does **yet** mean?

    a. but
    b. and
    c. so

14. a. In line 59, what are **microorganisms**?

    ____

    b. Why is **microorganisms** in parentheses?

       1. It is an example.
       2. It is a special word.
       3. It is a foreign word.

15. Read lines 64–65.

    a. What are **fossils**?

    ____

    b. How do you know?

    ____

• C. Information Organization

Read the passage again. Underline what you think are the main ideas. Then scan the reading and complete the following outline, using the sentences that you have underlined to help you. You will use this outline later to answer questions about the reading.

I. *Mars Observer* Mission

  A. Date:
  B. Purpose: to move into orbit around Mars and send new information back to Earth
    1.
    2.
  C. Outcome:

II.

  A. Date:
  B. Purpose:
  C. Outcome:

III. Data About Mars and Earth

  A. Age of Mars and Earth:

  B. Water on Mars and Earth:

  C. Conditions on Mars:

  D. Life on Earth:
    Life on Mars:

  E. Earth's Atmosphere:
    Mars' Atmosphere:

IV. Three Theories about Life on Mars

  A.
  B.
  C.

V. The Viking Landers Experiments

  A. Three Experiments:
  B. The Fourth Experiment:
  C. Results of all Four Experiments:

VI. Why Scientists Want to Investigate Mars Again

  A.

  B. They want to search for fossils.

VII. Questions That Scientists Want to Answer

A.
B.
C.

• D. Information Recall and Summary

Read each question carefully. Use your outline to answer the questions. Do not refer back to the passage. When you are finished, write a brief summary of the reading.

1. In the beginning, how were Earth and Mars similar?

____

____

2. How did Earth and Mars become different?

____

3. Describe the three theories about life on Mars.

   a. ______________________________

   ____

   b. ______________________________

   ____

   c. ______________________________

   ____

4. a. What tests did the Viking landers perform on Mars?

   ____

   b. What were the results of these tests?

   ____

5. Why do scientists believe that there are other areas on Mars that may support life?

____

6. What do scientists want to learn in the future?

____

Summary:

Work in pairs or alone. Write a brief summary of the reading, and put it on the blackboard. Compare your summary with your classmates'. Which one best describes the main idea of the reading?

____

____

____

____

____

• E. Word Forms

Part 1

In English, nouns change to adjectives in several ways. Some nouns become adjectives by adding the suffix *-al*—for example, *person* (n.) becomes *personal* (adj.).

Complete each sentence with the correct form of the words on the left. **Use the singular or plural form of the noun.**

experiment (n.)
experimental (adj.)

1. a. The design for a car that operates on solar energy is in the ______________ stage.
   b. Researchers will need to perform dozens of ____________________ to perfect this car.

environment (n.)
environmental (adj.)

2. a. Life can survive in hostile ______________, such as the black depths of the oceans.
   b. When ____________________ conditions change radically, some life forms die out.

development (n.)
developmental (adj.)

3. a. There are specialists in the field of psychology called ____________________ psychologists.
   b. These people study the complex __________ of humans from birth to death.

accident (n.)
accidental (adj.)

4. a. There was a fatal __________________ at the factory yesterday.
   b. The ____________________ explosion of a gas tank caused the death of three people.

function (n.)
functional (adj.)

5. a. The governor announced that the new power plant will be ______________ by next week.
   b. It will serve an important __________ as an extra source of energy.

Part 2

In English, adjectives change to verbs in several ways. Some adjectives change to verbs by adding the suffix *-ify,* — for example, *solid* (adj.) becomes *solidify* (v.).

Complete each sentence with the correct form of the words on the left. **Use the correct tense of the verb in either the affirmative or the negative form.**

intense (adj.)
intensify (v.)

1. a. A storm arose on the ocean and _______________ in severity. The captain of the ship bècame worried.
   b. He overcame his __________ feeling of fear and organized the crew to try to save the ship.

simple (adj.)
simplify (v.)

2. a. The college application form is not ___________________ enough, and many applicants fill it out incorrectly.
   b. As a result, the Admissions Office ___________________ the form in time for next term's applicants.

specific (adj.)
specify (v.)

3. a. Jeff is writing a beginner's cookbook, so his directions must be quite ___________________.
   b. If he ______________ exactly what to do, many beginners will become very frustrated.

clear (adj.)
clarify (v.)

4. a. Because the salesperson __________ the directions, Judy couldn't start up her new computer.
   b. She called the manufacturer, who sent an expert to give Judy __________ instructions, and she was able to begin working.

pure (adj.)
purify (v.)

5. a. When Fay and Ken go camping in the mountains next summer, they will not have any __________ water to drink.
   b. They __________ the water they find by boiling it for 20 minutes.

• F. Dictionary Skills

Read the following sentences. Use the context to help you understand the boldface words. Read the dictionary entry for that word and choose the appropriate definition. Then rewrite the sentence, using the definition you have chosen. Be sure to make your sentence grammatically correct.

1. Scientists lost **contact** with *Mars Observer* on August 24.

contact *n* **1** (state of) touching or communication; (process of) coming together. **2** business or social connection: *He made many business ~s while he was in Canada.* **3 (a)** connection (for electric current). **(b)** device for making this connection.

____

2. The spacecraft landed on Mars in order to search for any **signs** of life.

sign *n* **1** mark, object, symbol used to represent something: *mathematical ~s.* **2** word or words, design, etc. on a board or place to give a warning or to give directions: *traffic ~s.* **3** something that gives evidence, points to the existence or probability of something: *Are dark clouds a ~ of rain?* **4** movement of the hand, head, etc. used with or instead of words; signal. **5** symbol and name (often painted on a board) displayed by traders and storekeepers, etc. to advertise their business.

____

3. Scientists searched the rocks and frozen lakes of Antarctica. They found life forms that were **simple.** They hope to find such life forms on Mars.

simple *adj* **1** not mixed; not divided into parts; having only a small number of parts: *a ~ machine.* **2** plain; not much decorated or ornamented: *~ food/cooking.* **3** not highly developed. **4** easily done or understood; not needing great effort: *a ~ task.* **5** innocent; straightforward. **6** inexperienced; easily deceived.

---

4. Scientists want to land a spacecraft in a location that has more **promise** than the previous landing sites.

promise *n* **1** written or spoken undertaking to do, or not to do, give, something, etc. **2** that which one undertakes to do, etc. **3** indication or hope of success or good results.

• G. Vocabulary in Context

abundant (adj.)
arise (v.)
assumption (n.)
intriguing (adj.)
investigate (v.)
perform (v.)
similar (adj.)
support (v.)
survive (v.)
theory (n.)

Read the following sentences. Complete each blank space with the correct word from the list above. Use each word only once.

1. A human being can ____________ without food or water for several days, but will die within moments without air.

2. The police always __________ murders and robberies to try to find out who committed the crimes so they can arrest them.

3. Water is ___________ in many places, but it is rare in deserts.

4. In 1916, an astronomer named Percival Lowell had a ________ that there was a ninth planet, but Pluto was not discovered until 1930.

5. When Pat opened a letter from the college she had applied to, she began to cry. Susan was watching her and made the ___________ that the news was bad. Her guess was correct: Pat was not accepted by the college.

6. Many students do not _____________ well on examinations because they become very nervous and tense.

7. Fay suggested a two-month camping trip to the Himalayas next summer. Her husband Ken thought the idea was ___________. They had never done anything so exciting before!

8. Venus and Earth are _______________ in size. However, the surface temperature of Venus is 600 degrees Farenheit!

9. It is probably impossible for life to ever ______________ on Venus because of its intense surface heat.

10. Maria will attend college next semester, and her parents agreed to ________________ her, so she will not have to get a job.

• H. Topics for Discussion and Writing

1. Do you think there is life on another planet? Why or why not?
2. Do you think that life on Earth is simply an accident? Why or why not?
3. Do you think it is important for scientists to study other places in space? Explain your answer.
4. Does your country have a space program? If so, how would you compare it to the space program in this country?

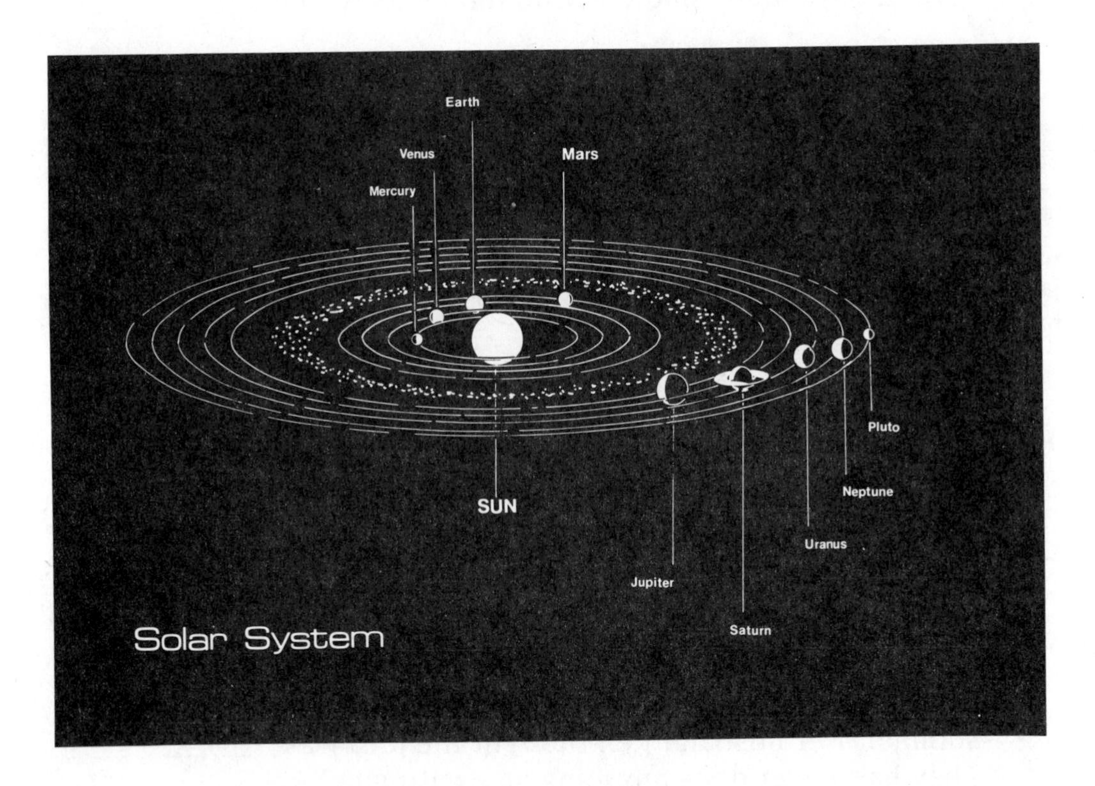

• I. Follow-Up Activity

Choose a planet in our solar system to read about. Prepare a report on the planet. Use the chart below to record your information. In class, work in groups of three. Discuss the planets you have chosen. Decide whether it is possible for life to exist on these planets. List your reasons. Compare your information with your classmates' information. As a class, decide which planets could possibly support life.

PLANET	DIAMETER AND DISTANCE FROM THE SUN	DESCRIPTION OF THE PLANET	REASONS WHY LIFE IS POSSIBLE	REASONS WHY LIFE IS NOT POSSIBLE
Mercury				
Venus				
Earth				
Mars				
Jupiter				
Saturn				
Uranus				
Neptune				
Pluto				

Unit IV Review

• J. Crossword Puzzle

1 2 3 4 5 6 7 8 9 10 11 12 13 14 15 16 17 18 19 20 21 22 23 24 25 26 27 28 29 30 31 32 33 34 35 36 37

Clues

Across

2. a sign
4. You will succeed ___ you work hard.
6. ask for information
7. surroundings; everything around you
11. I am going ___ eat lunch.
12. habit; usual behavior
13. room
14. soldier of fortune
17. I am ___ tired. I slept very well last night.
19. good, better; bad, ___
21. an Egyptial king
23. I am; we ___.
24. the past of *make*
25. unluckily
26. to learn very well; to become skilled at something
28. the past of *sit*
31. a test
34. the past of *have*
35. certainly; surely
37. an unproven idea

Down

1. find
2. to take over by force
3. the opposite of *yes*
5. in addition; moreover
8. This coat costs $2,000. It is ___ expensive.
9. a simple life form
10. burial place
15. dig up
16. An ___ is a person who studies the sun, planets, and stars.
18. the opposite of *down*
20. a belief
22. my, his, ___
27. not complex
29. tightly closed
30. the opposite of *succeed*
32. the opposite of *difficult*
33. this, that, ___, those
36. the opposite of *no*

• K. Unit IV Discussion

1. The three chapters in this unit discuss the uses of technology in solving problems related to the past, the present, and the future. What do you think are the most important problems science and modern technology should try to solve?
2. What can the past teach us about the present? How can this help us in the future?
3. How does technology help us today? Give specific examples.

Index of Key Words and Phrases

Pullout Section

Cloze Quizzes

• Chapter 1: A Cultural Difference: Being on Time

Read the passage below. Fill in the blanks with one word from the list. Use each word only once.

adapt	ended	instead	only
appointment	fact	late	punctual
behavior	formal	misinterpret	rude
contrast	greeted	neither	status
difference	hand	nor	unacceptable

1. ____________ 11. ____________

2. ____________ 12. ____________

3. ____________ 13. ____________

4. ____________ 14. ____________

5. ____________ 15. ____________

6. ____________ 16. ____________

7. ____________ 17. ____________

8. ____________ 18. ____________

9. ____________ 19. ____________

10. ____________ 20. ____________

In the United States, it is important to be on time, or (1)____________ , for an appointment, a class, a meeting, etc. However this may not be true in all countries. An American professor discovered this (2)____________ while teaching a class in a Brazilian university. The two-hour class began at 10 A.M. and (3)____________ at 12 P.M. One the first day, when the professor arrived on time, no one was in the classroom. Many students came after 10 A.M. Several arrived after 10:30 A.M. Two students came after 11 A.M. Although all the students (4)____________ the professor as they arrived, few apologized for their lateness. Were these students being (5)____________ ? He decided to study the students' (6)____________.

The professor talked to American and Brazilian students about lateness in both an informal and a (7)____________ situation: lunch with a friend and in a university class. He gave them an example and asked them how they would react. If they had a lunch (8)__________ with a friend, the average American student defined lateness as 19 minutes after the agreed time. On the other (9)__________ , the average Brazilian student felt the friend was late after 33 minutes.

In an American university, students are expected to arrive at the appointed hour. In (10)__________ , in Brazil, neither the teacher (11)__________ the students always arrive at the appointed hour. Classes not (12)__________ began at the scheduled time in the United States, but they also end at the scheduled time. In the Brazilian class, only a few students left the class at noon; many remained past 12:30 to discuss the class and ask more questions. While arriving late may not be very important in Brazil, (13)__________ is staying late.

The explanation for these differences is complicated. People from Brazilian and North American cultures have different feelings about lateness. In Brazil, the students believe that a person who usually arrives (14)__________ is probably more successful than a person who is always on time. In (15)__________ , Brazilians expect a person with (16)__________ or prestige to arrive late, while in the United States lateness is usually disrespectful and (17)__________ . Consequently, if a Brazilian is late for an appointment with a North American, the American may (18)__________ the reason for the lateness and become angry.

As a result of his study, the professor learned that the Brazilian students were not being disrespectful to him. (19)__________ , they were simply behaving in the appropriate way for a Brazilian student in Brazil. Eventually, the professor was able to (20)__________ his own behavior so that he could feel comfortable in the new culture.

• Chapter 2: Changing Lifestyles and New Eating Habits

Read the passage below. Fill in the blanks with one word from the list. Use each word only once.

alert	consequence	however	recent
along	consume	lifestyles	skip
average	example	nearly	survey
awareness	favorite	nutrition	threat
compile	habits	quantities	variety

1. ____________ 11. ____________
2. ____________ 12. ____________
3. ____________ 13. ____________
4. ____________ 14. ____________
5. ____________ 15. ____________
6. ____________ 16. ____________
7. ____________ 17. ____________
8. ____________ 18. ____________
9. ____________ 19. ____________
10. ____________ 20. ____________

Americans today have different eating (1)____________ than in the past. There is a wide selection of food available. They have a broader knowledge of (2)____________ , so they buy more fresh fruit and vegetables than ever before. At the same time, Americans purchase increasing (3)____________ of sweets, snacks, and sodas.

Statistics show that the way people live determines the way they eat. American (4)____________ have changed. They now include growing numbers of people who live alone, single parents and children, and double-income families. These changing lifestyles are responsible for the increasing number of people who must rush meals or sometimes (5)____________ them altogether. Many Americans have less time than ever before to spend preparing food. Partly as a (6)____________ of this limited time, 60% of all American homes now have microwave ovens. Moreover, Americans eat out (7)____________ four times a week on the (8)____________ .

It is easy to study the amounts and kinds of food that people (9)__________ . The United States Department of Agriculture (USDA) and the food industry—growers, processors, marketers, and restaurateurs—(10)__________ sales statistics and keep accurate records. This information not only tells us what people are eating, but also tells us about the changes in attitudes and tastes. Red meat, which used to be the most popular choice for dinner, is no longer an American (11)__________ . Instead, chicken, turkey, and fish have become more popular. Sales of these foods have greatly increased in (12)__________ years. This is probably a result of the (13)__________ of the dangers of eating food that contains high levels of cholesterol, or animal fat. Doctors believe that cholesterol is a (14)__________ to human health.

According to a recent (15)__________ , Americans also change their eating patterns to meet the needs of different situations. They have certain ideas about which foods will increase their athletic ability, help them lose weight, make them (16)__________ for business meetings, or put them in the mood for romance. For (17)__________ , Americans choose pasta, fruit, and vegetables, which supply them with carbohydrates, to give them strength for physical activity, such as sports. Adults choose foods rich in fiber, such as bread and cereal, for breakfast, and salads for lunch to prepare them for business appointments. For romantic dinners, (18)__________ , Americans choose shrimp and lobster. While many of these ideas are based on nutritional facts, some are not.

Americans' awareness of nutrition, (19)__________ with their changing tastes and needs, leads them to consume a wide (20)__________ of foods—foods for health, for fun, and simply for good taste.

• Chapter 3 Dreams: Making Them Work for Us

Read the passage below. Fill in the blanks with one word from the list. Use each word only once.

altogether	dream	negative	step
changing	gradually	next	therapy
charge	grown	positive	tired
cheerful	hard	recall	upset
continued	identify	simple	woke

1. ____________________ 11. ____________________

2. ____________________ 12. ____________________

3. ____________________ 13. ____________________

4. ____________________ 14. ____________________

5. ____________________ 15. ____________________

6. ____________________ 16. ____________________

7. ____________________ 17. ____________________

8. ____________________ 18. ____________________

9. ____________________ 19. ____________________

10. ____________________ 20. ____________________

Several nights a week Joseph (1)__________ up screaming from the same terrible (2)__________ . Joseph could never (3)__________ his whole dream, though. He only remembered that someone was running after him. He (4)__________ having this nightmare for months. He was so (5)__________ in the morning that it was (6)__________ for him to go to work. Joseph, you see, is not a frightened child, but a (7)__________ man.

Dr. Rosalind Cartwright has developed a dream therapy for (8)__________ dreams. According to Dr. Cartwright, dream therapy involves four (9)__________ steps you can learn on your own. The first (10)__________ is to recognize when you are having a bad dream that makes you feel helpless or (11)__________ the next morning. The second step is to (12)__________ what it is about the dream that makes you feel bad. (13)__________ , stop any bad dream. You do not have to continue your bad dream, because you are in (14)__________ . The last step is to change the (15)__________ part of the dream.

By using dream (16)____________ , Joseph was able to change his nightmares. (17)____________ , his bad dreams stopped (18)____________ . He began having more (19)____________ dreams and woke up feeling refreshed and (20)____________ . A night of good dreaming can leave us all in a better mood in the morning.

• Chapter 4: Language: Is It Always Spoken?

Read the passage below. Fill in the blanks with one word from the list. Use each word only once.

babies	innate	observations	resemble
capacity	language	over	same
consistent	learn	pattern	speech
deaf	matter	prefer	varied
example	movements	psychologist	words

1. ______________ 11. ______________

2. ______________ 12. ______________

3. ______________ 13. ______________

4. ______________ 14. ______________

5. ______________ 15. ______________

6. ______________ 16. ______________

7. ______________ 17. ______________

8. ______________ 18. ______________

9. ______________ 19. ______________

10. ______________ 20. ______________

Recently, doctors have learned that deaf (1)__________ babble with their hands. Laura Ann Petitto, a (2)__________ at McGill University in Montreal, Canada, has studied how children (3)__________ language. She observed three hearing infants and two (4)__________ infants. After watching and videotaping the children for several hundred hours, the psychologist and her assistants made many important (5)__________ . For (6)__________ , they saw that the hearing children made many different, (7)__________ motions with their hands. However, there appeared to be no (8)__________ to these motions. The deaf babies also made many different (9)__________ with their hands, but these movements were more (10)__________ and deliberate. The deaf babies seemed to make the (11)__________ hand movements over and (12)__________ again. During the four-month period, the deaf babies' hand motions started to (13)__________ some of the basic hand-shapes used in ASL. The children also seemed to (14)__________ certain hand-shapes.

Linguists—people who study language—believe that our ability for language is (15)__________ . In other (16)__________ , humans are born with the (17)__________ for language. It does not (18)__________ if we are physically able to speak or not. (19)__________ can be expressed in many different ways—for instance, by (20)__________ or by sign.

• Chapter 5: Loneliness: How Can We Overcome It?

Read the passage below. Fill in the blanks with one word from the list. Use each word only once.

chronic	instance	phenomenon	severe
circumstances	interests	popularity	shyness
connection	loneliness	predict	temporary
factor	normal	rational	unfortunately
habitual	overcame	remained	words

1. ____________ 11. ____________

2. ____________ 12. ____________

3. ____________ 13. ____________

4. ____________ 14. ____________

5. ____________ 15. ____________

6. ____________ 16. ____________

7. ____________ 17. ____________

8. ____________ 18. ____________

9. ____________ 19. ____________

10. ____________ 20. ____________

Most people feel lonely sometimes, but it usually only lasts between a few minutes and a few hours. This kind of loneliness is not serious. In fact, it is quite (1)____________. For some people, though, loneliness can last for years. Psychologists are studying this complex (2)____________ in an attempt to better understand long-term loneliness. These researchers have already identified three different types of loneliness.

The first kind of loneliness is (3)____________. This is the most common type. It usually disappears quickly and does not require any special attention. The second kind, situational (4)____________, is a natural result of a particular situation—for example, a divorce, the death of a loved one, or moving to a new place. Although this kind of loneliness can cause physical problems, such as headaches and sleeplessness, it usually does not last for more than a year. Situational loneliness is easy to understand and to (5)____________.

The third kind of loneliness is the most (6)____________. Unlike the second type, chronic loneliness usually lasts more than two years and has no

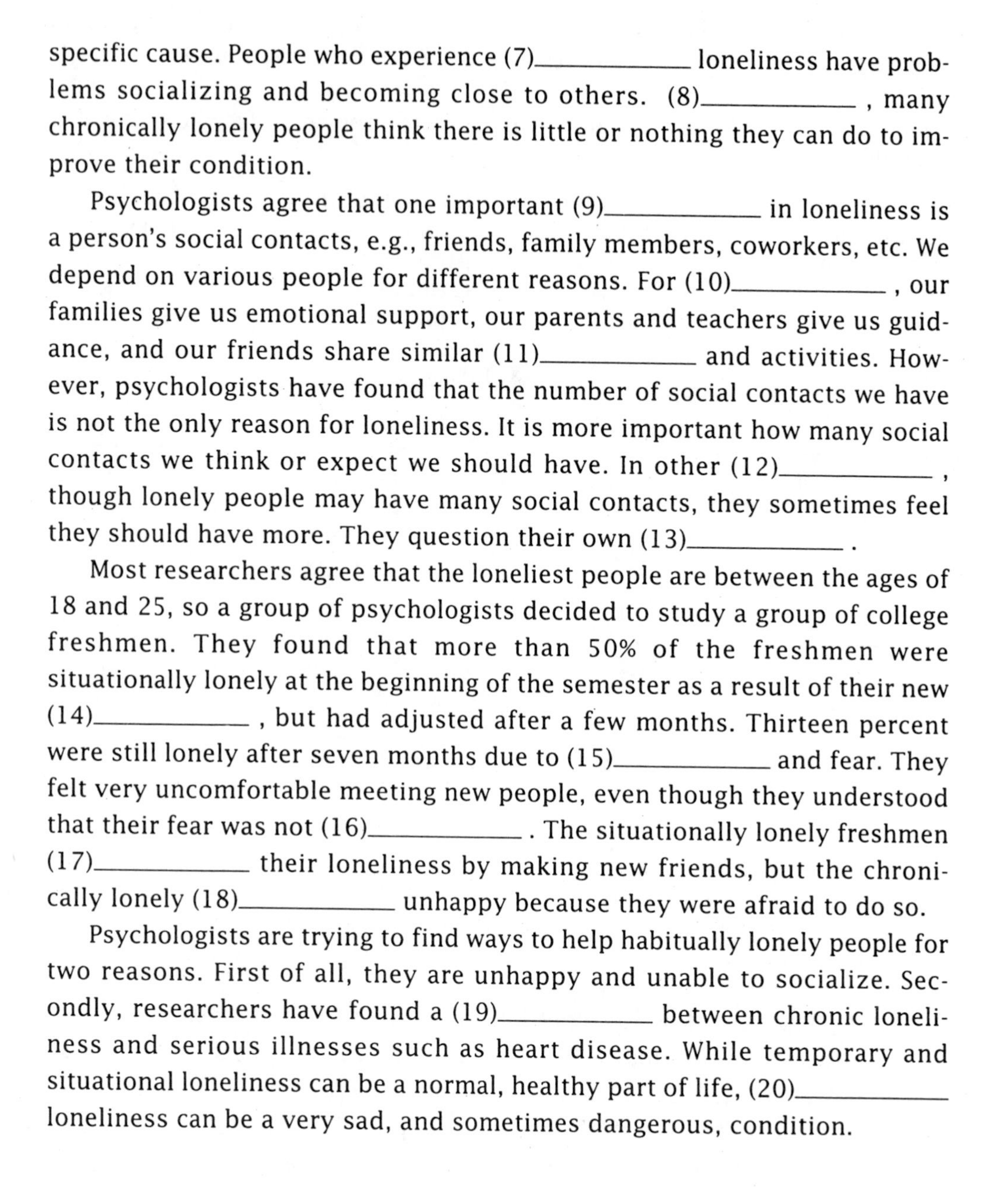

specific cause. People who experience (7)___________ loneliness have problems socializing and becoming close to others. (8)___________ , many chronically lonely people think there is little or nothing they can do to improve their condition.

Psychologists agree that one important (9)___________ in loneliness is a person's social contacts, e.g., friends, family members, coworkers, etc. We depend on various people for different reasons. For (10)___________ , our families give us emotional support, our parents and teachers give us guidance, and our friends share similar (11)___________ and activities. However, psychologists have found that the number of social contacts we have is not the only reason for loneliness. It is more important how many social contacts we think or expect we should have. In other (12)___________ , though lonely people may have many social contacts, they sometimes feel they should have more. They question their own (13)___________ .

Most researchers agree that the loneliest people are between the ages of 18 and 25, so a group of psychologists decided to study a group of college freshmen. They found that more than 50% of the freshmen were situationally lonely at the beginning of the semester as a result of their new (14)___________ , but had adjusted after a few months. Thirteen percent were still lonely after seven months due to (15)___________ and fear. They felt very uncomfortable meeting new people, even though they understood that their fear was not (16)___________ . The situationally lonely freshmen (17)___________ their loneliness by making new friends, but the chronically lonely (18)___________ unhappy because they were afraid to do so.

Psychologists are trying to find ways to help habitually lonely people for two reasons. First of all, they are unhappy and unable to socialize. Secondly, researchers have found a (19)___________ between chronic loneliness and serious illnesses such as heart disease. While temporary and situational loneliness can be a normal, healthy part of life, (20)___________ loneliness can be a very sad, and sometimes dangerous, condition.

• Chapter 6: Care of the Elderly: A Family Matter

Read the passage below. Fill in the blanks with one word from the list. Use each word only once.

advance	dependent	mutually	require
caregiving	elderly	obligation	responsibility
common	even	perhaps	siblings
consideration	eventually	reasons	spouse
cooperative	moreover	regardless	statistic

1. ____________ 11. ____________
2. ____________ 12. ____________
3. ____________ 13. ____________
4. ____________ 14. ____________
5. ____________ 15. ____________
6. ____________ 16. ____________
7. ____________ 17. ____________
8. ____________ 18. ____________
9. ____________ 19. ____________
10. ____________ 20. ____________

Who takes care of the elderly in the United States today? The fact is that family members provide over 80% of the care that elderly people need. Most times, the (1)____________ live in their own homes. A very small percent of America's elderly live in nursing homes.

Samuel H. Preston, a sociologist, studied how the American family is changing. He reported that by the time the average American couple reaches 40 years of age, their parents are usually still alive. This (2)____________ shows the change in lifestyles and responsibilities of aging Americans. The average middle-aged couple can look forward to caring for elderly parents some time after their own children have grown up. (3)____________ , because people today live longer after an illness than people did years ago, family members must provide long-term care. These facts also mean that after caregivers provide for their elderly parents, who will (4)____________ die, they will be old and may (5)____________ care too. When they do, their spouses will probably take care of them because they have had fewer children than their parents did.

Because Americans are living longer than ever, more psychologists and social workers have begun to study ways of (6)__________ to improve care of the elderly. They have found that all caregivers share a (7)__________ characteristic: All caregivers believe that they are the best person for the job, for different (8)__________ . One caregiver said that she had always been close to her mother. Another was the oldest child. Another was the youngest child. (9)__________ of the reason, the caregivers all felt that they could do the job better than anyone else. Social workers interviewed caregivers to find out why they took on the (10)__________ of caring for an elderly, (11)__________ relative. They discovered three basic reasons. Many caregivers believed that they had an (12)__________ to help their relative. Some stated that helping others made them feel more useful. Others hoped that by helping someone now, they would deserve care when they became old and dependent.

When people care for an elderly relative, they often do not use available community services, such as adult day-care centers. If the caregivers are adult children, they are more likely to use such services, especially because they often have jobs and other responsibilities. In contrast, a (13)__________ , usually the wife, is much less likely to use support services or to put the dependent person in a nursing home.

Researchers have found that caring for the elderly can be a very positive experience. The elderly appreciated the care and attention they received. They were affectionate and (14)__________ . However, (15)__________ when caregiving is satisfying, it is hard work. Social workers and experts on aging offer caregivers and potential caregivers help when arranging for the care of an elderly relative. One (16)__________ is to ask parents what they want before they become sick or dependent. (17)__________ they prefer going into a nursing home and can select one in (18)__________ . On the other hand, they may want to live with their adult children. Caregivers must also learn to be assertive and ask for help from others, especially (19)__________ . Brothers and sisters are often willing to help, but they may not know what to do.

We can expect to live longer lives than ever before in American history. Caring for the elderly and being taken care of can be a (20)__________ satisfying experience for everyone involved.

• Chapter 7: Innocent Until Proven Guilty: The Criminal Court System

Read the passage below. Fill in the blanks with one word from the list. Use each word only once.

appear	guilty	people	responsibility
consider	hears	protect	time
crime	however	prove	whether
defendant	innocent	punishment	witnesses
evidence	jury	purpose	words

1. ____________________ 11. ____________________

2. ____________________ 12. ____________________

3. ____________________ 13. ____________________

4. ____________________ 14. ____________________

5. ____________________ 15. ____________________

6. ____________________ 16. ____________________

7. ____________________ 17. ____________________

8. ____________________ 18. ____________________

9. ____________________ 19. ____________________

10. ____________________ 20. ____________________

The (1)__________ of the American court system is to (2)__________ the rights of the (3)__________ . According to American law, if someone is accused of a (4)__________ , he is considered (5)__________ until the court proves that the person is guilty. In other (6)__________, it is the responsibility of the court to (7)__________ that a person is (8)__________ . It is not the (9)__________ of the person to prove that he is innocent.

At a trial, a jury of 12 people listens to the (10)__________ from both attorneys and (11)__________ the testimony of the (12)__________ . Then the (13)__________ goes into a private room to (14)__________ the evidence and decide (15)__________ the defendant is guilty of the crime. If the jury decides that the (16)__________ is innocent, he goes free. (17)__________ , if he is convicted, the judge sets a date for the defendant to (18)__________ in court again for sentencing. At this (19)__________ , the judge tells the convicted person what his (20)__________ will be.

• Chapter 8: The Reliability of Eyewitnesses

Read the passage below. Fill in the blanks with one word from the list. Use each word only once.

appearance	evidence	instance	reliable
bitter	eyewitness	judges	similar
civilians	guilty	mistake	testimony
crimes	influence	occurred	victims
despite	innocent	questions	yet

1. ______________ 11. ______________

2. ______________ 12. ______________

3. ______________ 13. ______________

4. ______________ 14. ______________

5. ______________ 15. ______________

6. ______________ 16. ______________

7. ______________ 17. ______________

8. ______________ 18. ______________

9. ______________ 19. ______________

10. ______________ 20. ______________

Bernard Jackson is a free man today, but he has many (1)__________ memories. Jackson spent five years in prison after a jury convicted him of raping two women. Jackson's lawyer introduced witnesses who testified that Jackson was with them in another location at the times of the crimes. Why, then, was he convicted? The jury believed the (2)__________ of the two (3)__________ . They positively identified Jackson as the man who had attacked them. The court eventually freed Jackson after the police found the man who had really committed the crimes. Jackson was similar in (4)__________ to the guilty man. The two women had made a (5)__________ in identity. As a result, Jackson has lost five years of his life.

The two women in this case were eyewitnesses. They clearly saw the man who attacked them, (6)__________ they mistakenly identified an innocent person. Similar incidents have (7)__________ before. Eyewitnesses to other crimes have identified the wrong person in a police lineup or in photographs.

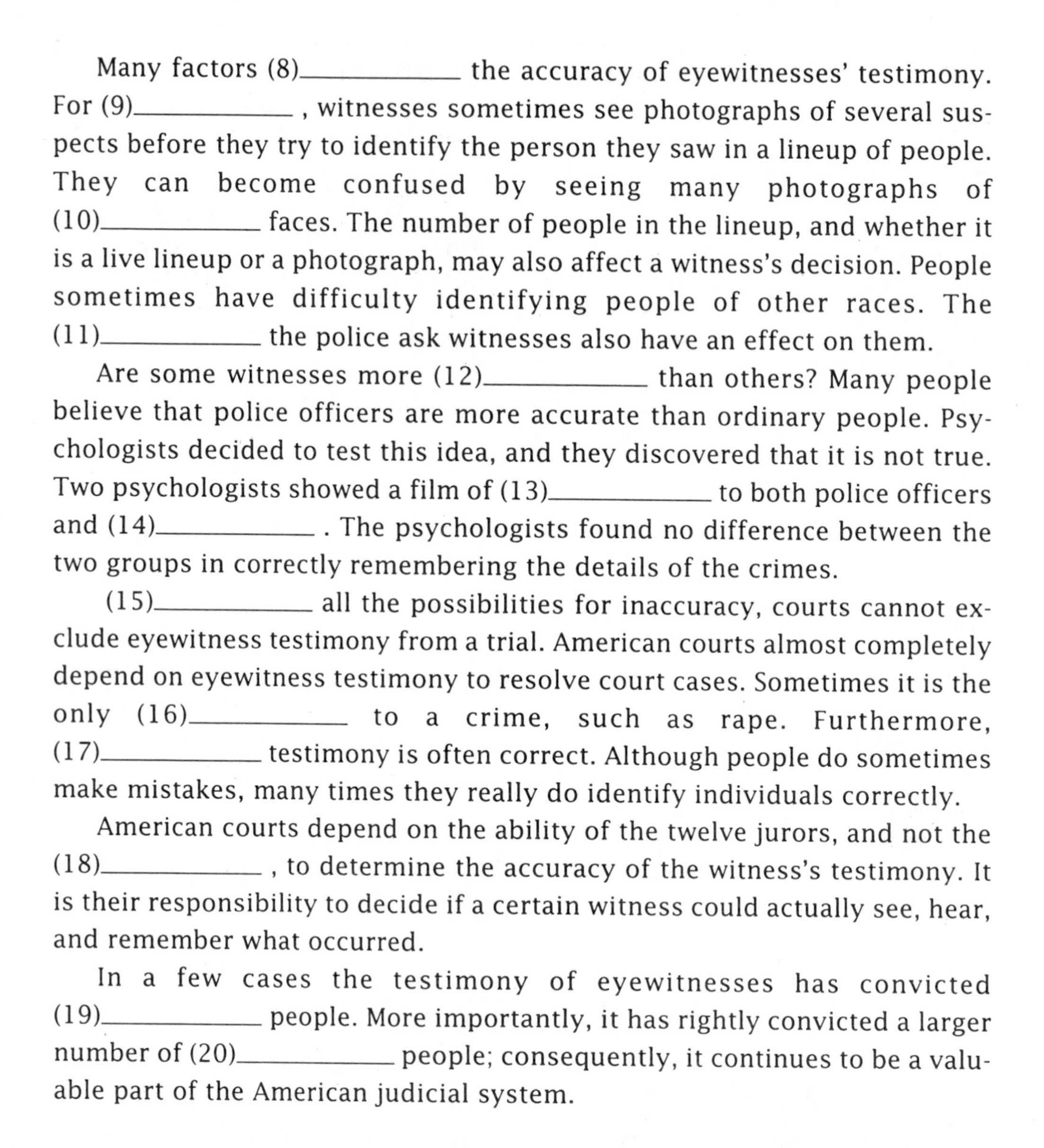

Many factors (8)__________ the accuracy of eyewitnesses' testimony. For (9)__________ , witnesses sometimes see photographs of several suspects before they try to identify the person they saw in a lineup of people. They can become confused by seeing many photographs of (10)__________ faces. The number of people in the lineup, and whether it is a live lineup or a photograph, may also affect a witness's decision. People sometimes have difficulty identifying people of other races. The (11)__________ the police ask witnesses also have an effect on them.

Are some witnesses more (12)__________ than others? Many people believe that police officers are more accurate than ordinary people. Psychologists decided to test this idea, and they discovered that it is not true. Two psychologists showed a film of (13)__________ to both police officers and (14)__________ . The psychologists found no difference between the two groups in correctly remembering the details of the crimes.

(15)__________ all the possibilities for inaccuracy, courts cannot exclude eyewitness testimony from a trial. American courts almost completely depend on eyewitness testimony to resolve court cases. Sometimes it is the only (16)__________ to a crime, such as rape. Furthermore, (17)__________ testimony is often correct. Although people do sometimes make mistakes, many times they really do identify individuals correctly.

American courts depend on the ability of the twelve jurors, and not the (18)__________ , to determine the accuracy of the witness's testimony. It is their responsibility to decide if a certain witness could actually see, hear, and remember what occurred.

In a few cases the testimony of eyewitnesses has convicted (19)__________ people. More importantly, it has rightly convicted a larger number of (20)__________ people; consequently, it continues to be a valuable part of the American judicial system.

• Chapter 9: The Death Penalty in the United States: Old Enough to Kill, Old Enough to Die?

Read the passage below. Fill in the blanks with one word from the list. Use each word only once.

allow	currently	minors	protect
appealed	execute	nonetheless	refused
committed	fear	opponents	sentenced
convicted	governor	perhaps	suggest
crimes	limit	proponents	that

1. ______________________ 11. ______________________

2. ______________________ 12. ______________________

3. ______________________ 13. ______________________

4. ______________________ 14. ______________________

5. ______________________ 15. ______________________

6. ______________________ 16. ______________________

7. ______________________ 17. ______________________

8. ______________________ 18. ______________________

9. ______________________ 19. ______________________

10. ______________________ 20. ______________________

In the United States, 36 states (1)__________ allow capital punishment for serious crimes such as murder. Americans have always argued about the death penalty. Today, there is a serious question about this issue: should there be a minimum age limit for executing criminals? In other words, is it right for convicted murders who kill when they are (2)__________—i.e., under the age of 18—to receive the death penalty?

In most other countries of the world, there is no capital punishment for minors. In the United States, though, each state makes its own decision. Of the 36 states that (3)__________ the death penalty, 30 permit the execution of minors.

In the state of South Carolina, a (4)__________ murderer was given the death penalty for a crime he committed while he was a minor. In 1977, when he was 17 years old, James Terry Roach and two friends brutally murdered three people. Roach's lawyer fought the decision to (5)__________ him. The young murderer remained on Death Row (a separate part of prison for convicted criminals who are sentenced to die) for ten years while his lawyer (6)__________ to the governor. The lawyer argued that it is wrong to execute a person for a crime he committed while he was a minor. In the United States, the (7)__________ of a state has the power to change a sentence from the death penalty to life in prison. (8)__________, the governor of South Carolina (9)__________ to stop the execution. Roach was finally executed by electrocution in 1986. This is not the first time a criminal was executed in South Carolina for a crime he (10)__________ when he was a minor. In 1944, a 14-year-old boy died in that state's electric chair.

In Indiana, a 16-year-old girl was on Death Row for a crime she committed when she was 15. Paula Cooper and three friends stabbed an elderly woman to death in 1986. They robbed the old woman to get money to play video games. At the time of the murder, the minimum age (11)__________ for executions in that state was 10. Cooper's lawyer appealed to the governor of Indiana to stop the execution because the convicted killer was very young and because she was abused in childhood. The Indiana governor, who favors the death penalty, said (12)__________ he had to let the courts do their job.

Two years after Paula Cooper's crime, Indiana raised the minimum age limit for executions to the age of 16. However, the courts still refused to stop Cooper's execution because she had been (13)__________ before the age limit for executions was changed. In 1988 the U.S. Supreme Court decided to bar, or prohibit, the execution of juveniles who were under the age of 16 when they committed their crime. Cooper's lawyer again asked the court to stop her execution. Finally, in July of 1989, Paula Cooper was sentenced to 60 years in prison. She is no longer on Death Row.

Although no one believes that these killers deserve sympathy, some people believe that capital punishment is too severe for convicted murderers who are minors. They feel that it is wrong to treat minors the same as adults in these cases. (14)__________ of the death penalty in general think it is wrong to take one life for another. They argue that capital punishment does not (15)__________ the victim or the victim's family. Opponents also (16)__________ that, occasionally, innocent people may be executed for (17)__________ they did not commit.

On the other hand, people who agree with the death penalty argue that it prevents repeat crimes and, therefore, future victims. These (18)__________ of capital punishment believe that (19)__________ of the death penalty deters crime. That is, fewer people will commit murder because they fear the death penalty.

The laws concerning capital punishment are changing every day. (20)__________ in the future other states will change their laws, as Indiana did. In the meantime, though, the controversy continues.

• Chapter 10: Ancient Artifacts and Ancient Air

Read the passage below. Fill in the blanks with one word from the list. Use each word only once.

addition	compare	excavations	museum
air	crypt	fact	predict
although	custom	however	recover
ancient	discovery	information	sealed
chamber	examining	king	so

1. ______________________ 11. ______________________

2. ______________________ 12. ______________________

3. ______________________ 13. ______________________

4. ______________________ 14. ______________________

5. ______________________ 15. ______________________

6. ______________________ 16. ______________________

7. ______________________ 17. ______________________

8. ______________________ 18. ______________________

9. ______________________ 19. ______________________

10. ______________________ 20. ______________________

Archeologists made an exciting (1)____________ in Egypt in 1954. During an excavation near the base of the Great Pyramid, they uncovered an ancient crypt. Although they believed that this discovery would help us understand Egypt's past, they also hoped that it would give us important (2)____________ about the future.

This (3)____________ was a tomb, or burial place, for a dead Egyptian pharaoh, or (4)____________ . Historians believed that the Egyptians buried their pharaohs with two boats: one to carry the body and another to carry the soul. This was one of their religious customs about death. The archeologists expected to find two boats inside the crypt. As they broke the crypt open, they smelled the scent of wood. The ancient Egyptians had sealed the room so effectively that the aroma of the cedar wood was still preserved. Inside the crypt, archeologists found a 4,600-year-old boat that was in almost perfect condition. In (5)____________ , they found another closed room next to the crypt. Archeologists and historians believed that this chamber contained the second boat. If (6)____________ , archeologists would have

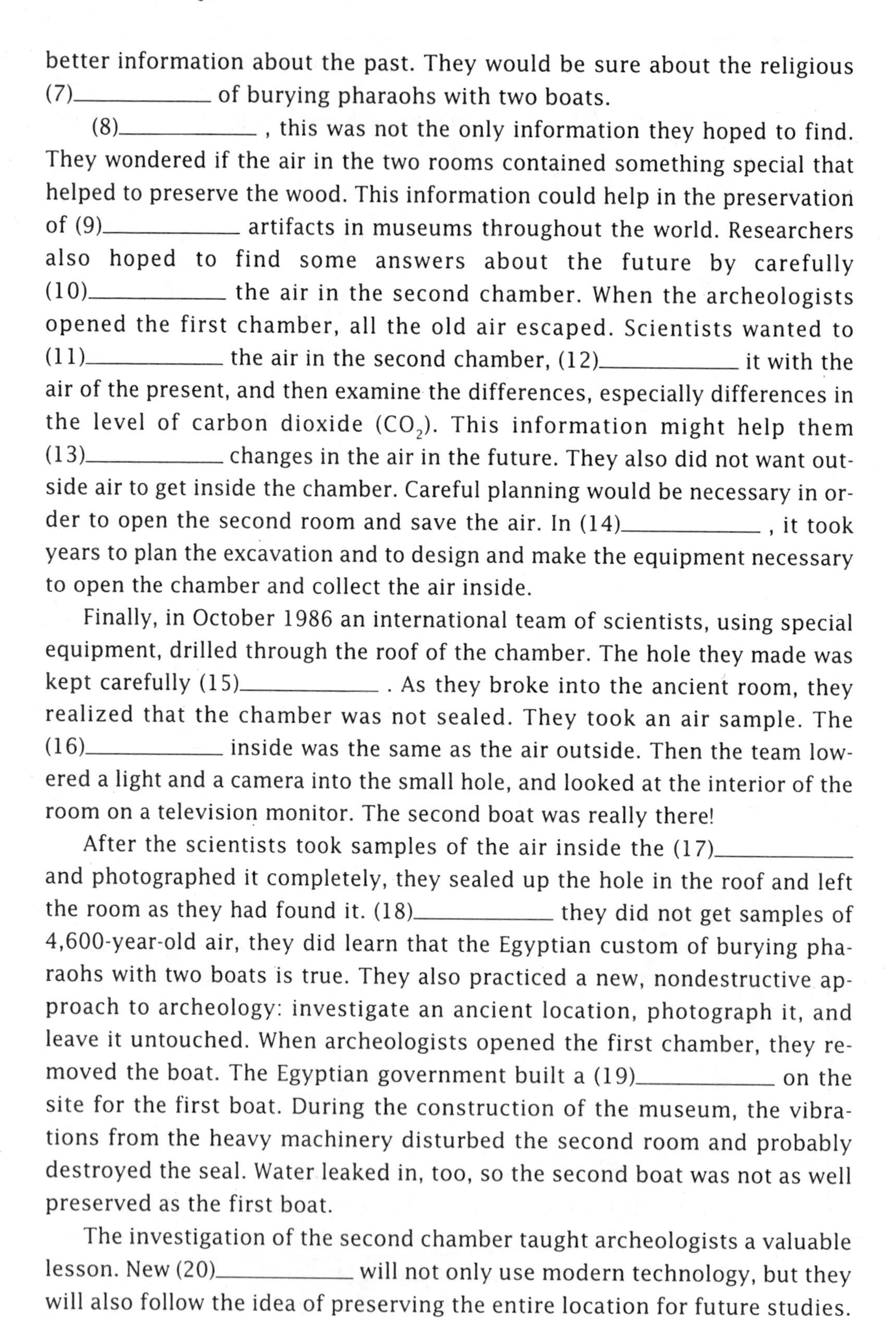

better information about the past. They would be sure about the religious (7)__________ of burying pharaohs with two boats.

(8)__________ , this was not the only information they hoped to find. They wondered if the air in the two rooms contained something special that helped to preserve the wood. This information could help in the preservation of (9)__________ artifacts in museums throughout the world. Researchers also hoped to find some answers about the future by carefully (10)__________ the air in the second chamber. When the archeologists opened the first chamber, all the old air escaped. Scientists wanted to (11)__________ the air in the second chamber, (12)__________ it with the air of the present, and then examine the differences, especially differences in the level of carbon dioxide (CO_2). This information might help them (13)__________ changes in the air in the future. They also did not want outside air to get inside the chamber. Careful planning would be necessary in order to open the second room and save the air. In (14)__________ , it took years to plan the excavation and to design and make the equipment necessary to open the chamber and collect the air inside.

Finally, in October 1986 an international team of scientists, using special equipment, drilled through the roof of the chamber. The hole they made was kept carefully (15)__________ . As they broke into the ancient room, they realized that the chamber was not sealed. They took an air sample. The (16)__________ inside was the same as the air outside. Then the team lowered a light and a camera into the small hole, and looked at the interior of the room on a television monitor. The second boat was really there!

After the scientists took samples of the air inside the (17)__________ and photographed it completely, they sealed up the hole in the roof and left the room as they had found it. (18)__________ they did not get samples of 4,600-year-old air, they did learn that the Egyptian custom of burying pharaohs with two boats is true. They also practiced a new, nondestructive approach to archeology: investigate an ancient location, photograph it, and leave it untouched. When archeologists opened the first chamber, they removed the boat. The Egyptian government built a (19)__________ on the site for the first boat. During the construction of the museum, the vibrations from the heavy machinery disturbed the second room and probably destroyed the seal. Water leaked in, too, so the second boat was not as well preserved as the first boat.

The investigation of the second chamber taught archeologists a valuable lesson. New (20)__________ will not only use modern technology, but they will also follow the idea of preserving the entire location for future studies.

• Chapter 11: How Lunar Eclipses Have Changed History

Read the passage below. Fill in the blanks with one word from the list. Use each word only once.

ability	eclipses	however	succeed
advantages	enemy	omen	take
again	for	only	thick
attacked	furthermore	prediction	time
capable	helpless	repaired	unfortunately

1. ______________________ 11. ______________________

2. ______________________ 12. ______________________

3. ______________________ 13. ______________________

4. ______________________ 14. ______________________

5. ______________________ 15. ______________________

6. ______________________ 16. ______________________

7. ______________________ 17. ______________________

8. ______________________ 18. ______________________

9. ______________________ 19. ______________________

10. ______________________ 20. ______________________

Lunar eclipses have always fascinated people. Some study eclipses as an astronomical phenomenon; others just enjoy observing their beauty. However, in ancient—and even in more recent—times, lunar (1)__________ were mysterious, unpredictable, and frightening. In the past, people believed that eclipses were bad omens, or signs, and this superstition has often affected historical events. (2)__________ instance, a lunar eclipse was partly responsible for the fall of Constantinople in 1453.

Constantinople was named for the Roman emperor Constantine, who moved his capital to Byzantium (present-day Istanbul in Turkey) in 324 A.D. The Byzantine government ruled the area for over a thousand years.

In the 15th century, the Ottoman (Turkish) Empire was planning to (3)__________ over Constantinople. The Turkish troops attacked Constantinople in 1402 and (4)__________ in 1422, but did not (5)__________ . Then in 1451, sultan Mohammed II (6)__________ the city again. Mohammed II had several (7)__________ over the defenders of the city. For instance, he had 250,000 men in his army; Constantinople was fortified by (8)__________ 7,000 troops. The sultan also had a new style of cannon that shot stones weighing 1,300 pounds. This weapon was (9)__________ of breaking through Constantinople's (10)__________ walls. In April 1453, the Turkish army attacked the city's thick walls with its new cannon. The defenders, however, (11)__________ the walls every night. (12)__________ , they attacked back several times. Still, after some (13)__________ , the 7,000 defenders became exhausted. They never thought of giving up, (14)__________ , because they had faith in an old prophecy. The (15)__________ stated that Constantinople could never fall while the moon was becoming full. (16)__________ , on May 22, 1453, the full moon went into an eclipse. The defenders felt frightened and (17)__________ . Three days later, Mohammed II attacked the city again. In a very short time, the Turkish army overpowered Constantinople's troops. Constantinople's defenders had believed the evil (18)__________ about the moon; the lunar eclipse made them feel that the battle would be hopeless, and they lost their (19)__________ to protect their city from the (20)__________ .

Chapter 12: Mars: Our Neighbor in Space

Read the passage below. Fill in the blanks with one word from the list. Use each word only once.

abundant	experiments	locations	similar
arose	fossils	performed	support
assumption	intensified	planet	survived
conditions	intriguing	possibility	theories
contrast	investigation	protects	unfortunately

1. ______________	11. ______________
2. ______________	12. ______________
3. ______________	13. ______________
4. ______________	14. ______________
5. ______________	15. ______________
6. ______________	16. ______________
7. ______________	17. ______________
8. ______________	18. ______________
9. ______________	19. ______________
10. ______________	20. ______________

Astronomers all over the world were waiting in excitement as August 1993 approached. *Mars Observer*, the American spacecraft, was scheduled to move into orbit around Mars. In addition to mapping the (1)__________, *Mars Observer* was going to study the Martian atmosphere and surface. (2)__________, scientists lost contact with *Mars Observer* on August 24.

In (3)__________, the United States' previous mission to Mars in 1976 was a great success. Two American spacecraft landed on Mars in order to search for signs of life. The tests that the Viking landers (4)__________ had negative results. However, scientists still had questions about Mars. They wanted to investigate further into the (5)__________ of life on Mars.

Scientists' interest in the Red Planet is based on an (6)__________. They believe that 4.5 billion years ago, Mars and Earth began their existence under (7)__________ conditions. During the first billion years, liquid water was (8)__________ on the surface of Mars. This is an indication that Mars was much warmer at that time. Mars also had a thicker atmosphere of carbon dioxide (CO_2). Many scientists think it is possible that life began under these favorable conditions. After all, Earth had the same conditions during its first billion years, when life (9)__________. At some point in time, Earth developed an atmosphere that is rich in oxygen, and an ozone layer. The ozone layer (10)__________ Earth from harmful ultraviolet light from the Sun. While life not only began on Earth, it also (11)__________ and became more complex. In contrast, Mars lost its thick atmosphere of carbon dioxide. Ultraviolet radiation (12)__________. The planet grew colder, and its water froze.

A biologist at NASA, Chris McKay, has suggested three (13)__________ about life on Mars. One possibility is that life never developed. A second possibility is that life arose during the first billion years, but did not survive. The third is that life arose and simple organisms developed. When environmental (14)__________ on Mars changed, life ended.

The two Viking landers performed four (15)__________. Three experiments tested for biological activity in the soil. The fourth experiment looked for evidence of life. All the tests were negative.

Scientists were dissatisfied because the two sites where the Viking spacecraft landed provided safe landing places, but they were not particularly interesting (16)__________. Scientists believe there are other areas on Mars that are similar to specific places on Earth that (17)__________ life. For example, an area in Antarctica, southern Victoria Land, which is not covered by ice, resembles an area on Mars. In its dry valleys, the temperature in southern Victoria Land averages below zero, yet biologists found simple life forms. Perhaps this is also true of places on Mars.

Scientists want another (18)__________ of Mars. They want to map the planet's surface and land a spacecraft in a more promising location. They want to search for (19)__________, the ancient remains of life. If life ever existed on Mars, scientists believe that future missions might find records of it.

Even if future missions discover no evidence of past or present life on Mars, scientists will look for the answers to other, (20)__________ questions. How is Earth different from Mars? How can we explain the development of life here on our planet and not on Mars, our close neighbor? Are we alone in the universe?